ON MY OWN

ON MY OWN

Personal Independence for Today's Woman

by Greta Walker

WILLIAM MORROW AND COMPANY, INC.

New York 1980

Library of Congress Cataloging in Publication Data

Walker, Greta.
  On my own.

  1. Women—Conduct of life.   2. Single women—
Conduct of life.   3. Women—Psychology.
4. Self-actualization (Psychology).   5. Success.
I. Title.
HQ1221.W23   158'.1   79-27917
ISBN 0-688-03664-3

Printed in the United States of America

First Edition

1   2   3   4   5   6   7   8   9   10

Book Design by Michael Mauceri

Acknowledgments

My deepest thanks to Virginia Barber and Pat Golbitz for their help and support, to Naomi Cutner for her kindness and hard work, and to Ellyn Polshek for encouraging me to find my own voice.

A special thanks to all the women who have participated in my workshops, who have shared their lives with me, and have allowed me to share my life with them.

Workshop I

We sit in a circle in the plant-filled room of a New York City women's center. There are seven of us: the six workshop participants and I, the leader. Our subject: women on their own. This is the first of five two-hour sessions. The women have signed up for the workshop as a result of an ad that reads: "Do you feel only half a person if you don't have a lover or a husband? Do you think single women are lonelier than married women?" They have all put down on their applications that they don't feel whole; to be single is to be lonely. They hope that during the five sessions they will learn things that will help them feel differently. I hope so, too. That's the purpose of the workshop.

We start off by introducing ourselves and giving some background material. I go first. I tell them my name is Greta Walker, I'm fifty-one, I was married for seventeen years, and I've been single for the past five years. I have a seventeen-year-old son. I explain that up until very recently I was convinced that I was only complete as part of a couple. "I never saw myself as a whole, separate person with ideas and feelings of my own. I assumed my sense of self came from that magical other person. Without him I was nothing."

The women nod. They know exactly what I'm talking about.

I continue: "For that reason I always kept a man in my life. My marriage was miserable from the beginning, yet I hung in there. I'd think of leaving, but when I'd look around there was never another man I wanted to leave for. How could I give up what I had? I certainly couldn't make a life all by myself. What would I do as a woman alone? Who would want to have anything to do with me?"

One of the women interrupts me: "It's hard to believe you were like that. You seem so strong."

"I know," I respond. "Isn't it crazy? I was strong then, too, but I sure as hell didn't know it. I had no idea I could make a life for myself. It's true I had a sort of career as an actress, and toward the end of my marriage I had a sort of career as a writer, but I never 'went for broke' with either of them. Nothing should interfere with my staying close to my husband and child. I didn't want to take a chance on their finding someone else if I weren't around."

I go on to explain that, finally, in the sixteenth year of my marriage, I became so wretched that I knew I had to do something. "So I went to a psychotherapist and asked her to please help me make my marriage better. Her reply was that she couldn't help me change my marriage, but she could work with me to try to help me change myself so that I'd be better equipped to make happier choices. I didn't have to go on being so miserable.

"That was a bit of a letdown. Changing *myself* wasn't exactly what I had in mind. At that point, however, I was desperate. Besides, I had a good feeling about this woman. I sensed there was much I could learn from her. I was right."

I recall for the women an eye-opening conversation I had with the therapist. During one session I had asked her if she had ever been married, and she had answered, "Yes, for eight years." Then I had asked her if she had found going through a divorce very painful. In her usual forthright manner, she had replied that it had been just awful. It had been especially hard because she hadn't yet developed her techniques for working through such a difficult emotional transition. When I asked her if she ever thought of getting married again, her reply had been prompt and very sincere: "Absolutely not. I love my life. I love living alone."

"Her answer knocked me out," I tell my listeners. "I had

never dreamed a woman would *choose* to live alone. I understood that you should make the best of the single years, but always with your focus on finding a man so you could once again be complete. And now this terrific woman was telling me she already felt complete. She was genuinely pleased with her life exactly as it was. What a revelation! I had more than one option! I didn't have to leave one man and go to another. I could go forth as a woman alone. And, after a year of many vacillations and tears and fears, that's exactly what I did."

I make it clear to the women that the last five years have not been easy—in fact, at times enormously painful. But I also make it very clear that the results have been well worth the struggle. "Being on my own," I say, "has opened up my life in ways I never dreamed possible.

"I started giving these workshops two years ago because I wanted to share with other women some of the ideas and techniques that helped me change from a dependent, anxious, frustrated woman to an independent person who can handle anxiety, who can deal with frustration, and who has learned to find pleasurable alternatives to the depressing choices I used to make. I'm not a therapist, and I can't help you make miraculous transformations—nobody changes miraculously anyhow—but I hope that as a result of our discussions here you'll begin to think about your lives in different, more innovative ways. Please understand," I add, "that I don't have all the answers, even though I have a tendency to sound as though I do." The women laugh and I laugh, too, for I'm aware that I often get carried away by my convictions. I continue: "What I'm giving you are some ideas and suggestions that have worked very well for me and for many other women. If you can adapt these things to your own lives, wonderful. If not, perhaps just being exposed to some new thoughts will help you come up with ideas of your own."

Finally, I assure the women that I'm not advocating that

we should all renounce men, that *I* certainly haven't. But I *am* advocating feeling good about ourselves, taking responsibility for ourselves, enjoying ourselves whether there's a man in our lives or not.

When I've finished speaking, I suggest we go around the circle and that each woman give her name, some information about herself, and tell us what she hopes to get out of the workshop.

The blond woman on my left, who looks no more than eighteen, speaks first. Her voice is automatic and flat, her pretty face devoid of much expression other than a compliant smile. She informs us her name is Susan and she is thirty —we all stare at her in disbelief. She was married for seven years and has been divorced for three. She had been living with her present boyfriend for two years.

"I work for a large corporation as a secretary," Susan continues. "My boss wants to help me move ahead in the company, but somehow I can't get any enthusiasm for it. I know I should. I don't want to be a secretary the rest of my life. The place where I work is great. They'll send me to school so I can get the skills and degree I need for promotion. The trouble is, I never get around to enrolling. Isn't that dumb?" Wide, innocent, blue eyes sweep the circle, and I'm getting the message she doesn't think it's so dumb.

Susan sighs and goes on: "It's hard for me to do things. My husband always did everything for me, and now my boyfriend does everything for me. I wouldn't have come to the workshop, even though I wanted to a lot, if a girlfriend of mine who took your last workshop hadn't sat me down and made me write the check. She even sent the check off for me. I did manage to get here all by myself, though." She blushes prettily. We all laugh.

Susan concludes by saying that she would like to take more initiative and not be so dependent. She wonders if I have some suggestions as to how she should start. She looks at me with those large, expectant, cornflower-blue eyes, and

I have the uncomfortable feeling she would like me to take over her life for her just as her husband, boyfriend, girlfriend, and boss have done. I caution myself against falling into the trap.

I tell Susan that over the five weeks I'll be able to throw a little light on why she doesn't do more for herself, and I'll even suggest a few beginning steps she might follow. But I emphasize that ultimately she's going to have to do the nitty-gritty work on her own. "Your strength will come from testing yourself in all sorts of situations. As long as you don't do anything, you'll never know what you *can* do. You're going to have to show yourself that you have skills and capabilities."

She looks blank, and I hasten to add that I realize she's completely unused to doing for herself and that it will take a lot of practice to begin to feel comfortable. I ask her if her mother and father did a lot for her.

"Everything," Susan answers. "I never had to lift a finger." She smiles sweetly at the recollection.

"No wonder it's so hard for you to take control of your life. You've had a lot of years of being done for." She sighs again. I wait for her to say something, but she has lapsed into silence. I hope that means she's thinking about what I've said.

The woman to the left of Susan is a picture of quiet understatement: chin-length, straight brown hair; brown and beige sweater and skirt; brown, medium-heeled shoes; one simple gold chain around her neck.

"My name is Julia and I'm forty-six," she begins in a voice that is almost inaudible. I ask her to please speak up so we can all hear her.

She continues in a louder tone, and we learn that she was married for twenty-three years, has been widowed for three years, and that she has a twenty-one-year-old daughter and a nineteen-year-old son. The rest of her story is a familiar widow's tale: the perfect marriage of two loving, inseparable people; the inability to feel whole, even after three years, without a man. "I have no ambitions or desires anymore," she confides. "I know I have to find someone else and get married again. But it's so hard to meet a man. I've gone to all those dreary singles' places and they only depress me. I thought maybe in the workshop I'd get some ideas from the other women as to how to go about meeting someone."

I repeat to her that the purpose of the workshop is to help women view themselves as whole persons whether they're with a man or not. "Maybe some of the women can be helpful in directing you toward places to meet men," I add, "but I'd like to focus elsewhere. You haven't mentioned your work. What do you do and how do you feel about it?"

"I'm a bookkeeper and I hate it." No need to ask her to speak up now.

"Is there something else you'd like to do?"

"I don't know what I want. Nothing seems to give me pleasure."

I tell her I understand her feelings because I went through a similar joylessness when my marriage broke up. "But," I say, "one thing that helped give shape and interest to my life was my work. To continue in a job you hate is to work against yourself. You've tried the quest for a man and it hasn't done much for you, so why not try something different? How about giving serious thought to finding a more interesting career?"

"It never occurred to me I could change careers."

"I don't see why you can't. At least you can think about some other possibilities. Then you'll be dealing with substance, something you can have some control over. Getting involved in work can make you feel good about yourself. But if you depend on another person to give you self-esteem, to infuse your life with meaning, you'll always be on shaky ground. If that person dies or leaves, you're back to zero again."

Julia replies that she never thought of herself as someone who could function alone, and I suggest that she use the
five sessions to explore exactly what she can do on her own—
in all areas, not just in work. "If you meet a man you like and
want to marry, wonderful," I add. "But whether you meet
someone or not, at least you'll have pursuits and interests
that are important to you. I find that by going in that direction, I've lost the desperate, anxious, clutchy feeling I used
to have."

Julia shrugs. She looks perplexed and annoyed. All she
had wanted were five easy ways to meet a man, and I'm giving her complicated things to think about. But, I remind myself, that's what I'm here for.

I swing my eyes to the woman next to Julia, whose exotic features are framed by masses of frizzy jet-black curls.
She begins to talk immediately. Her words tumble out one
on top of the other, punctuated by the constant motion of
long, awkward hands.

"My name is Laura and I'm thirty-eight and I've never
been married. I'm a secretary but I want to get married but
it doesn't seem to be happening. I'd like to have a baby and
I've thought if I didn't get married I could get pregnant and
raise a child alone but that scares me." She pauses to catch
her breath and looks vaguely around the circle. "I don't
know why I came to the workshop but I thought I might get
some ideas."

When I ask her how she feels about her secretarial job,
she wrinkles her nose in distaste and tells me she doesn't like
it very much. She only stays because the benefits are good.

Has she ever thought she might find a job she liked that
offered similar benefits?

No. She guesses she mostly assumes she'll get married, and
then she'll quit. She laughs nervously. "I guess I'm pretty
confused. I have this boyfriend who treats me really awful
and yet I can't break with him. If he doesn't call, and lots of

times he doesn't, I feel like I hardly exist. I don't know why
I don't break up with him." The nervous laugh again. "Maybe he'll change, I don't know."

I point out that she's doing a lot to make her life harder
than it need be. She's staying with a job she doesn't like and
a man who makes her unhappy. "You do have other options,"
I tell her, "even though they're not apparent to you. There's
no rule that says you have to endure things that make you
miserable. Do you ever think about why you hang onto these
things?"

"Yeah, I do think, sometimes." Again the vague look. Then
she says, almost defensively, "I'm afraid to give anything up.
Boyfriends are hard to come by at my age. I think about getting a better job but my mother keeps telling me that I'm
crazy to go anywhere else and that I'll never find such good
benefits. Maybe she's right. Besides, she really wants me to
get married."

"You're thirty-eight years old. You're old enough to make
your own decisions. You don't have to live your life on your
mother's terms."

"Tell my mother that," Laura retorts. Suddenly she declares that she doesn't want to talk anymore.

I start to reply that *she* could tell her mother, but I stop
myself. It's never that easy. Instead I say, "Okay. Maybe
you'll feel more like talking later." I look to the next woman,
a very young, slim, stylishly dressed brunette.

"My name is Connie," she begins. "I'm twenty-four, I'm
single, and I've never been married. I have a good job as a
sportswear buyer for a department store. My work is no
problem—I love it and I do well at it. I have a lousy boss, but
I think I can handle that. My big problem is finding a man I
like. All the guys I become involved with turn out to be such
male chauvinists."

The other women register amazement that even young
men are still stuck in the old attitudes toward women. Only
Julia challenges her.

"I don't see how there can be any problems at your age," she blurts out. "You can pick and choose. At my age there are so few choices."

"There may be more choices for me," Connie answers her, "but that doesn't make it any easier to find someone who treats you as an equal. I think it's very hard at any age."

"When I was in my early twenties, there were all kinds of men I could have married," Julia persists with some bitterness. "Now there is no one."

"Maybe you were looking for different things then."

"Maybe," Julia concedes.

"Anyhow," Connie continues, "I've come to the workshop hoping to find out if there are things I can do to get a man to treat me with more respect."

I explain that I can't give a formula for changing the men in her life, but I can outline what motivates us to pick certain kinds of people. That could shed light on why she's drawn to "macho" men, even though she claims she wants a different kind of man. I can also discuss how our search for the perfect relationship makes it doubly hard to form a relationship between two separate, imperfect people. "Let's face it," I say, "close relationships are very difficult, and when we approach them with all sorts of unreal expectations and demands, they can't help but disappoint us. I'm not implying that's what you do," I say to Connie, "but it's certainly a prevalent attitude and it's worth talking about."

The fifth woman in the circle is well dressed and well coiffed and sports some elegant and expensive jewelry. She informs us her name is Elaine, that she's fifty-five, and then surprises us with the fact that she's married. "I've been married twenty-eight years." Her quavery voice indicates she's ready to cry. "I know the workshop is for women alone . . . but I think I belong here." Her voice breaks. She stops talking and looks down at her lap. We wait quietly. When she raises her head, her eyes are full of tears. With great effort she says: "I feel . . . very alone these days." Again her gaze goes to her lap. Connie places a comforting hand on her arm while the rest of us look on compassionately. Haven't we all known her despair at one time or another?

When she has sufficiently recovered, Elaine goes on with her story. Her daughter, with whom she was exceedingly close—they did everything together—recently married and moved with her husband to New Mexico. "So far away," Elaine laments. Her husband, with whom she was never very close, has become even more distant. "He told me he's tired of going to concerts and parties with me," she reveals. "He has no interest in traveling. He only wants to play golf with his buddies from the club. He says I can do anything I want and he'll pay for it, but he . . . doesn't want to go with me." Once more her eyes become watery pools.

I ask her how she feels the workshop can help her.

"I'd like to know how I can persuade my husband to do things with me," she pleads, wiping her eyes with a tissue. "What can I do? It wouldn't be so hard if my daughter were still here. I don't see why they had to move so far away."

"I wish I could give you a method for changing your husband," I answer regretfully, "but I can't. He's the only one who can make changes in himself, and it sounds as though he's pretty set on what he wants. And I can't tell you how to bring your daughter back, nor should that be one of your goals; she's entitled to a life of her own. I can only encourage you to begin to approach your life differently. For example, start by thinking about your marriage: How do you feel about it? What pleasures does it give you? What are its disadvantages? Once you've evaluated it, you can decide if you want to stay in it—*as it is*. You might conclude that you want out. Or, if you decide you want to stay, then you should give some thought as to what you can do within the reality of your situation—that means without your husband's participation. Maybe finding some interesting work would be part of your decision. Once you start weighing and comparing and thinking, you'll begin to come up with various alternatives."

Elaine stares at me helplessly. "I don't see that I have alternatives. At my age, I can't suddenly leave my husband and get a job. I've never worked in my life, except as a volunteer. What would I do? And who's going to do things with me? All my women friends have husbands who like to be with them."

I quickly assure her that I'm not suggesting she take any drastic action. My only recommendation is that she look to herself for answers, rather than to her husband and daughter. I add that I'm fully aware that it's not an easy task, but my experience has shown me that there's no other way that really works. I also remark that she shouldn't automatically rule out a job. "I interviewed a career counselor," I say, "who was quite optimistic about women in their forties and fifties entering the labor force. She claimed she's not yet met a woman who, with some digging, couldn't come up with skills and experience that could qualify her for a job. So work could be an option. So could doing things with a group, or even alone. There *are* alternatives."

Elaine nods and blows her nose.

It occurs to me that Elaine is a perfect example of how marriage is no long-range solution to the problem of what to do with your life. I say to the group: "I'm glad we have a married woman in the workshop because she illustrates that, married or single, we're all in the same boat. *Our* lives are *our* responsibilities, and there's no getting away from it. The married woman can be totally involved with husband and children for a number of years, but sooner or later, just like the single woman, she has to come to terms with the fact that she is a separate, alone person."

Julia grimaces. "You make it sound so awful." Everyone laughs.

I laugh, too. "It's really the reverse of awful. I've found

that as I've taken on more responsibility, I've been able to have better relationships with men *and* women. I'm freer to pick and choose. I can get together with someone because I like the person and want to be with him or her, not because I feel needy."

We've come to the last person in the circle—a slightly plump, lively woman of thirty-seven. Her name is Ann. She has been divorced for four years, has no children, and works in public relations. Ann claims she hasn't come to the workshop because she has any problems, but simply out of curiosity. "I like to meet new people," she states. "My life is very full. I'm always on the go, and I have lots of interesting friends." She doesn't want to talk about herself right now, but she does want to ask a question.

"Ask away."

"You keep talking about working things out alone," Ann observes. "Don't you believe in people helping each other, in working things out together? Whenever I have problems I immediately call one of my friends. They do the same with me. We're always there for each other. You seem to advocate such a solitary way of life."

I say: "I'm sorry if I gave the impression that everything should be done alone. That's not what I meant. I have many friends who have been extremely kind and helpful to me. And I've been helpful to them. That means a lot to me. This workshop is far from a solitary endeavor. But I do feel strongly that you shouldn't turn your life over to someone else. If, every time you have trouble, you depend on a friend to bail you out, you're not free. And, in fact, that's what we're hearing tonight. Almost all the women have expressed helplessness, loneliness, a sense of nothingness, without another person to make them complete."

I go on to explain that I feel most complete when I use my abilities and my intelligence to the fullest, without running to someone else. "It's very strengthening to sit down and think a problem through on your own, and then to come up with a plan of action. It's very exciting, albeit a little scary, to analyze and evaluate and then to take a risk on your judgment. Even when you make a mistake, it's never *that* upsetting. It's *your* mistake and you can learn from it."

I look at Ann. "Does that answer your question?"

"Sort of. Let me think about what you've said."

Now that we've introduced ourselves, I ask the women if there are any comments or questions.

Elaine observes that it's good to be able to talk to a group of women and wishes it were easier to talk to men.

Laura echoes her sentiments and wonders why men have things so easy and women have such hard times. The other women take up the topic, and I can see we're about to get off on a woman-versus-man discussion. I interrupt with the opinion that, to my knowledge, men have problems and anxieties just as women do. "It doesn't do us much good to spend our time envying them or speculating on whether their problems are as great as ours. Let's just handle our lives and let the men handle theirs."

Susan asks me to pursue the subject I mentioned earlier—why we often gravitate toward people and situations that make us unhappy.

I agree and start by commenting on what I've picked up during the introductions. "Most of you said you want one thing," I say, "but you always end up with something quite different. Take you, Susan. You told us you want to do more for yourself, yet you never do. Connie maintains she wants a man who respects her but always finds herself with just the opposite. Laura's boyfriend, job, and mother give her no pleasure, still she keeps herself involved with them. In my case, for seventeen years I asserted that I wanted a relationship that had kindness and consideration as its components, yet stuck with a hate-filled marriage. I continually said I wanted to be financially independent but never took steps to put myself in that position. What I'm illustrating is that very often our *stated* goal is one thing, while our *real, unstated* goal is something quite different."

Susan looks puzzled. Her face has taken on a liveliness, and her voice has lost much of its early-evening flatness. "Why would we *want* to do things that don't give us pleasure?"

"Because it's all we know. In your case, although it doesn't give you much satisfaction and probably a lot of anxiety to depend on everyone else for the smallest things, it's familiar. You've been dependent all your life. There are no surprises when you let others take over, no risks. So you keep doing what you consider to be safe and comfortable. Comfortable, however, doesn't mean painless.

"I'll take it one step further. Not only is the repetitive behavior familiar, we also think we need it in order to survive. That's why it's so hard to give up. It starts when we're very small; our parents let us know—sometimes directly, sometimes just by insinuation—that we'd better act in certain ways or we'll be in real trouble. Since we're helpless and completely dependent on them, we interpret their message to mean they will abandon us if we don't toe the line. Therefore, we do whatever we think they want of us, even if it's not in our best interest. We see it as a matter of life and death.

"The trouble is, the behavior becomes ingrained; as years go by it becomes so automatic that most of the time we're not conscious of what we're doing. As adults, without realizing it, we continue to gravitate to people who interact with us much as our parents did. Even though our survival is no longer an issue, we somehow believe it is. And so we keep doing the same dumb things over and over again, never perceiving that we can make other choices."

Connie wonders how one stops the "dumb things."

"First you have to recognize you're not a victim," I say, "that many of the happenings in your adult life occur through your unconscious choices. That involves carefully examining what you've been doing. Ask yourself why it is you say you want one thing and invariably end up with something else. What are you doing that always guarantees the same results? Go through the probing until you can establish for yourself that you're controlling things much more than you ever thought.

"The second step is to decide if you would like to change so you could make better conscious choices—let's face it; not everyone wants to make changes. If you decide in favor of change, you can go on to the third step. There you try to understand that your repetitive behavior comes from the survival kit you set up as a child. You do that by comparing the similarities between your present close relationships and the relationship you had with your parents. That can be tricky because we don't always see our parents too clearly. So we have to struggle to come up with a true picture of them as opposed to our fantasy of them. As the past comes into focus, and we observe how it matches up with the present, we're able to recognize that those behavior patterns are unnecessary, even harmful, to us as adults. We're no longer dependent children who need others for survival. Once that is clear, we can take the next step which involves making efforts to stop the old ways. Again, not easy. It means listening to ourselves, catching ourselves in our automatic responses, and then consciously stopping ourselves. In the last step, we try out new, less familiar choices to see that we don't die, that we actually begin to live."

I emphasize that obviously the process of change doesn't go forward in neat steps. It's an up-and-down, back-and-forth procedure. "Some people make large changes—which is what I feel I've been doing—while others prefer to work on small areas of their lives. Sometimes you'll change one thing, and it will be so exciting that you'll become eager to work on something else. We'll go into this more fully during our remaining sessions."

Susan speaks: "I've never been able to say no to people. I don't understand why I can't. Like yesterday, my boyfriend said he wanted to come with me to my girlfriend's house next week, and I immediately said yes. But I didn't really want him to come. Did my saying yes have something to do with what we're talking about?"

I answer that although she doesn't want him to come, she seems to have an even stronger need not to oppose him —apparently not to oppose anybody since she claims she *never* says no.

Susan nods vehemently. "It's true. I always think something awful will happen if I refuse anybody anything."

"Which is what we've been talking about. If you say no, it might be the death of you—that could partially explain why you pretend you can't do very much; that way, people won't make too many demands on you, and you won't feel compelled to say yes so often. Think about this business of not being able to say no in terms of the steps I outlined. Notice if you pick people who expect you to be compliant. Are they like your parents in some way? You could learn a lot about yourself just by exploring this one pattern."

I then suggest that all the women start to observe themselves in order to see how they, too, behave in very automatic ways.

Finally, I add: "Here's something interesting I've learned that might help you, Susan, and the rest of you as well: It's okay to change your mind."

"It's a woman's prerogative," Ann chimes in brightly.

"Damn right," echoes Laura. "So why don't I ever use it?"

I say to Laura: "You probably feel as I did. I always thought that once you agreed to something, you couldn't go back on it. Well, I've made the big discovery that you can. So if you automatically say yes, and you realize later that you really didn't want to say yes, you can go back to the person and explain that you made a mistake—you want to say no. And guess what? Nobody drops dead."

And that's the last word. The session is over.

Out in the street, the women go off together toward a coffee shop. They have become friends already. I know from past workshops that several of the friendships will endure beyond the five weeks.

I walk alone up Madison Avenue, enjoying the crisp January air and the gorgeously decorated windows that line the street. I pass a well-dressed couple and notice that the woman's arm is securely tucked in the man's. I smile to myself. Five years ago I would have been overcome with envy. Tonight I'm too busy with my thoughts to have time for envy. I go over the events of the evening in detail. I think about the individual women. I roughly outline some of the ideas I want to cover the following week—I'll make notes when I get home. Perhaps next week I can give more illustrations of how we do the same dumb thing over and over. I remind myself to discuss the myth of the perfect relationship; the women had expressed interest in that. And I do want to discuss some of the women with my therapist. She has been truly helpful over the two years that I've been conducting the workshops, not only in supporting many of my observations and ideas, but in providing insights that I've overlooked. Moreover, she's not above pointing out those times when I could have handled a situation better.

When I first thought of the workshop, I had asked my therapist if she felt I was qualified. "After all, I don't have a Ph.D. in psychology," I had worried.

"You're not setting yourself up as a psychotherapist," she had replied. "You just want to share some things that you've learned in therapy and in your everyday life that have helped you. I think it's an excellent idea. You've made some significant changes in the past four years, and you have a solid understanding of how those changes came about. You're more than qualified to give a workshop."

And so I started, first with single large workshops—sixty to seventy women—and then graduated to smaller ones that ran for five sessions. I have never been bored with them or tired of doing them. Through those sessions I have gained new respect for women and their struggles to take control of their lives. Furthermore, I've been very gratified because many of the women have been able to put some of my suggestions to practical use. Others have offered helpful ideas of their own. Through the workshops friendships have been made, horizons expanded, risks taken. Working with the women and exploring the pattern of my own life have shown me without a doubt that, to varying degrees, we all have more options than we think we have; and that it's within the realm of possibility to find those options and to follow them.

One can change. And that's what this book is all about.

Chapter I

In one week it will be our wedding anniversary. I
don't know what we have accomplished in this one
year together. Sometimes it seems we have only
been destructive toward each other, and that it
would be best to break up. Tonight it seems quite
hopeless. We keep on having the same fruitless mis-
understandings that are never resolved. I'm afraid
to make the decision to leave, and yet I feel it's
wrong to put so much energy into something that
doesn't have much chance of success.
—From my journal, December 6, 1957

I remember the day my husband moved out. It was in
January 1974—a moderately cold New York City day. He
and a hired mover loaded his desk, typewriter, and desk
chair (the latter a gift from me), the hi-fi equipment, two
living-room chairs, a lamp, pictures, a bench, a double
dresser, an oak washstand and a small oak chest, some dishes
and glassware, and all his toilet articles and clothes into the
van.

It had been a sort of last-minute, haphazard kind of
dividing things up, even though we both had been antici-
pating this day for several months.

"Here, you'd better take half the wine glasses," I had said
impulsively as he was piling things into boxes. We barely
looked at one another, each of us preoccupied with the
frightening prospect of an unfamiliar future—perhaps a life
alone.

"I'd like to take the walnut marble-top chest in the bed-room," he suggested.

I stiffened. "You can't take that. Don't you remember how I worked for weeks to refinish it? You did nothing to help."

He was clearly disappointed. "You're right. I'll take the double dresser. But the Chinese rug is mine. My father gave it to us."

"I don't care." (And I meant it.) "Take it." I pulled out sweaters, underwear, gloves, and scarves from my side of the double dresser.

"And I'd like the painting in the dining room—the one Donna painted for us."

I couldn't protest since Donna had been his friend before mine, but I would miss that painting. It had been with us for fifteen years, and I had never tired of looking at it, had grown to love it. "Yes," I said, "you have a right to it." I couldn't watch as he lifted the large canvas with its brilliant splashes of color—I had never been able to decide if they depicted a flaming waterfall or flashes of light in a tempestu-ous sky—and handed it to the mover.

Neither my husband nor I mentioned the oak bar, yet I knew we both remembered the day we bought it as one of the few joyful days of our life together. We were on Second Avenue in the Nineties when I spotted the piece in an an-tique shop window. I called to my husband and son who were emerging from the pet shop across the street. The proprietor of the store explained that he couldn't get the bar out of the window to show us, but he would demonstrate its efficiency while we peered through the window. Outside, with faces pressed against the glass, we were joined by a policeman and a man playing the accordion—both could have come out of a play by Saroyan.

The five of us watched with rapt attention as the man in the window lifted the top of the bar to reveal a marble shelf and then pulled out a smaller shelf that was obviously meant to hold glasses.

"Isn't that something!" exclaimed the policeman. The man with the accordion played a lively tune to show his delight. Next, the store owner opened the drawer of the bar and closed it. With a flourish, he produced a long, ornate key from his pocket, waved it in the air, inserted it into the large keyhole of the drawer, and with a grand gesture locked the drawer. This theatrical demonstration was followed by an equally theatrical unlocking of the glass doors below. Behind the glass doors were a place for liquor and a glass shelf to hold still more glasses. We onlookers widened our eyes and made o's with our mouths to show that we were properly impressed.

The proprietor signaled the end of the demonstration, and the policeman and the accordion player followed us into the cluttered, musty store to kibitz while we closed the deal. Sixty dollars, one of the best buys we ever made. My husband and I had held hands as we left the store.

The memory saddened me. Its specialness pointed up once again the meagerness of my long marriage. How awful that I had stayed in it for so many years. How insane that I had felt I needed it so desperately. For almost two decades I had almost obliterated my real self in order to maintain a status quo. I had tried to be the perfect wife and mother: to intuit my husband's and child's every need; to always be there; to wait on them; to assuage their anxieties. Being married gave me status, I had thought. It made me superior to all those single women. I wouldn't do anything to jeopardize it. I recalled flashing my wedding ring—my status symbol—at the slightest provocation. I remembered removing it for the last time; reluctantly I had slipped off the small gold band and had gazed with pity at my naked, unimportant ring finger.

My husband's voice interrupted the recollection. He was talking of books and records: "We'll divide them when I get my shelves built. You *do* know that most of them are mine."

"Yes, I know." He could have them. I would start from

scratch and buy just the things I wanted.

After all the objects had been decided upon, and my husband and son had made their private and tearful farewell, there was nothing more to be said and done. It was all over. An awkward good-bye, a slam of the door, and he was gone.

My twelve-year-old son stayed in his room, and I sat in the living room, that was bare at one end and heavy with furniture at the other, and felt as if everything were tilting toward the windows. I stared at the naked picture hooks and the clean white squares where paintings had been hanging only a few minutes ago. I spoke aloud, my voice flat, dead: "It's over. There's no turning back. It's all over."

There was no emotion. And no wonder. There had been so much pain involved in deciding to separate. For one year I had tried to find the courage to make the break. There had been tearful appointments with lawyers, long, anguished talks with supportive friends and my therapist—"How do you know I can survive on my own?" "I know you can. You're stronger than you think you are. You've been making all the major decisions for years, you just haven't realized it." "But won't I die of loneliness?" "You'll be lonely, but you won't die; and it will get better." The worst part had been the wakeful nights where I conjured up hideous images of myself as a woman without a man.

Once the decision was made, there were the months of living the false family life while waiting for the signing of the separation agreement. Holidays had been the hardest. We had sat round the Thanksgiving table, the attractive nuclear family—the three of us tense, making small talk, forcing down forkfuls of turkey and stuffing, mother and father blotting out the scene with too many glasses of white wine. Christmas had been no better, with a nine-foot tree that none of us felt like decorating and token gifts exchanged between two hostile adults. Now there was nothing left but a numbing relief that it was finally over.

I walked through the apartment—my apartment. The

study was bare, waiting for me, the new tenant, to move in. I wondered anxiously if I would ever become worthy of a room of my own. Settling for a corner was more my style. In the bedroom my footsteps clicked on the bare floor now that the plush Chinese rug was gone. No matter. The floor was shining and beautiful. My clothes from the double dresser were strewn upon the bed and chairs and would have to be squeezed into the already full walnut chest. It seemed a simple task but I couldn't face it; not yet. I opened the second closet—totally empty. How wonderful! I could spread out.

Indeed, I was beginning to have a sense of space. Yes, everything was out of balance, in some places depressingly bare, but there was less clutter. There was room to breathe, to expand.

Shortly after my husband moved out on that Saturday in January 1974, I walked back into the living room and realized I couldn't bear another hour of a room that tilted precariously. If my life was momentarily off center, at least my surroundings should have some stability. I called some friends from the building and asked them if they would please come down and help me. They were at my door in minutes.

We pushed the upright piano a little to the left, the rocking chair to the end of the room opposite the window, the couch a bit to the right (how shabby it looked, and now there would be no money to slipcover or reupholster it). The easy chair with the hassock seemed out of proportion for the room in its present state. I would have to accept it until I could afford to replace it—prickles of fear along my spine let me know that I wasn't too sure I'd ever be able to afford it. How much had I earned last year—four thousand dollars? I didn't want to think about it.

After the rearranging, the room was far from perfect, and I still had to look at exposed picture hooks. But the dizzying quality had abated, and with a few plants and some inexpensive prints to cover up white spaces the room would be livable.

Next, feeling like an interloper in my husband's territory, I helped my friends carry my desk, typewriter, and filing cabinets from the bedroom to the study. The desk, smaller than my husband's, looked peculiarly dwarfed and forlorn against the long, white wall. It would take time to make the space my own. It would also take time to know if I could function as a writer without my editor-writer husband. It was he who had urged me to take up writing when I stopped acting, and it was he who decided when a piece of work was good enough to leave our house. I had relied on him completely, had been so fearful of being found inept that I wouldn't even submit a query letter without his pronouncing it fit to be read. I could feel the prickles along my spine again. Now I was alone.

When our work was finished, my friends and I sat in my newly balanced living room and made desultory conversation. I was aware they were pleased to help me through this period of transition, but I just wanted to be alone. It was too difficult to make small talk, and at that moment I didn't want to explore future plans. Sensing this, they soon left.

My son came out of his room. He appeared as drained of emotion as I. "Let's go to the movies," he suggested. "We should see *Magnum Force*. I think you'll like it."

"That's a crazy idea. I'll hate it."

"No, you'll see, you'll like it."

Well, I didn't like it, but it was a good idea. Two hours of Clint Eastwood and violence drowned out all thoughts of past sorrows and future problems. My son looked at me with amusement and some embarrassment as I gasped with horror at each successive atrocity.

But inevitably we had to go back to an apartment that seemed huge, silent, and strangely unfamiliar. Reluctantly my son went to sleep, and I, empty and heavy-limbed, rearranged the drawers of the walnut chest to accommodate the extra clothes. Later, surrounded by darkness, lying in the very center of my double bed—no more curling up in a ball on the edge of the left side to avoid the outstretched arms and legs of my husband—I wearily told myself that at last I could begin to refashion my life.

I was right to be weary, for time has shown me that lives don't refashion easily, not when you carry the baggage of your forty-six years along with you. It's a long, hard battle. There are days of feeling a failure, of wondering if you'll ever have any effect on the events that shape your existence; there are moments of terror when you're sure the gods will smash you for daring to assert yourself; and there are times when you just want to give it all up.

But I have kept at it. And I have never regretted the decision to go it on my own. In the five and a half years since my marriage ended, as I have worked to free myself of old attitudes and behaviors, there have been exciting results. I've become bolder and stronger; options I never thought I had have opened up for me. I'm earning a living, making important decisions, taking my own needs seriously. I've learned how to be a parent, a friend, someone who can give love and receive it. Best of all, I've learned to love myself. My life is more interesting, more varied, and far more rewarding than it ever was when I was a married lady proudly flashing her wedding ring.

And it can only get better.

Chapter II

What a crazy business is life. The hardest time for me is when I'm doing my own thing. Then I'm filled with such anguish I could cry. I become so frightened, so frantic that I keep reaching out for someone, anyone. I think this fear has held me back in realizing my own ambitions. As soon as I start to work on my behalf, I become panicked; I'm moving away from my moorings. If I go too far, stay away too long, maybe my moorings will be gone when I come back. I feel I must hold onto them at all costs.
—From my journal, August 24, 1959

In the weeks following the separation, I kept busy, so there was little time for introspection. I gave dinner parties, visited art galleries, went to concerts and movies. I was continuing the familiar, comfortable routines. Some of the people I knew went out of their way to include me in social events, although there were many long weekends where I ached for companionship—this was not such a new experience, since my marriage had contained many long, lonely weekends during which my husband and I had gone our separate ways. Moreover, I was able to remind myself that now I didn't have the resentment and anger that often accompanied the loneliness.

I was fortunate to have one friend in my apartment house who had separated from her husband two years before. She was enormously generous with her support and encouragement, both before and after my own separation, and almost daily we shared the travails of blessed singleness. Today

we look back with some amusement on those months of
tears and commiserations—it was not uncommon for one of
us to appear at the other's door and burst into sobs—and
our endless discussions of whether we would survive financially. But at that time our anxieties were all too real and
frightening. Neither of us was receiving magnificent sums
in alimony and child support, and both of us would have
to more than double our present sources of income if we
were to meet our expenses.

There were other women friends as well, and frequently
I found myself at parties—rather than flirting with men
(there weren't so many that one wanted to flirt with)—involved in long discussions with women about books, careers,
and, as ever, how we could make more money.

In truth, earning a living was, and still is, one of my major
concerns. I envied those women who had started their careers
in their twenties and now in their forties were vice presidents
of large companies, editors, psychotherapists, producers,
lawyers, doctors. Here I was at forty-six only just beginning
to build a career. How long would it take? Could I even do
it? I had such a low opinion of my own capacities, I wasn't
at all sure.

At the time, I had a contract for a young-adult book (my
first book, and interestingly it was to contain ten profiles of
contemporary women who had built worthwhile careers),
but the advance was very small, and so I began to take on
article assignments as well. I was astonished that I had the
ability to tackle more than one project. Before the separation,
I had assumed the book would be as much as I could handle
for a year, but here I was dividing my time among several
projects, as well as taking care of the house and trying to
keep up with the responsibility of being a single parent.

I was still terrified, however, of sending in work without
the approval of another person, so I quickly transferred my
dependence from my husband to a few women friends who
were writers and editors. I was constantly running over to

them with bits of unfinished copy. If my work wasn't well received, I'd be crushed. If I thought a piece of criticism was hostile, I'd feel enraged and helpless. If there was a positive response, I would be emboldened to write a few pages more. It was becoming increasingly clear that such dependence was only making me more insecure, and if I was ever to have any confidence about my work I was going to have to start making my own evaluations and decisions. Even if it meant appearing inept and foolish to editors, it was a risk I had to take.

The first article I turned in without asking help from anyone else was a piece on young widows for a physicians' magazine. How I agonized over it. I rewrote it dozens of times, then went over it again and again deleting extraneous phrases, trying to find the perfect words for each sentence. Desperately I wanted to run to friends for advice, and just as desperately I fought the impulse. When I finally sent the article off to my agent, it was with a sense of doom. Her voice on the phone a few days later started me trembling, and I awaited her negative verdict. "Hey," she said, "this piece is the best thing you've written. What happened?"

But did I dance for joy? Not at all. It was a fluke, I thought, a bit of luck not likely to be repeated. Her approval did give me courage to continue to rely on my own judgment, but at that time, and for a long time after, I couldn't believe that I had any control over what I produced. I wrote like an automaton, joylessly, and with no feeling that I was a professional who could make decisions and turn out work of merit. Often I would look back on an article and wonder how I had done it—it was almost as if the piece had been written by somebody else. Still, I was functioning, and I was bringing in a small amount of money, which was certainly a step in the right direction.

If my writing was moving along somewhat, my work as a parent was not keeping pace; much easier to have an impact on a blank piece of paper than to confront a twelve-year-old boy who has learned to disregard everything you say. When I look back on that period, all I can remember are the sneering challenges from my son: "You can't make me do that. What will you do if I don't?"

What *would* I do? I didn't know. I had seldom ever made him do anything; he had always gotten his way by wheedling or having a tantrum. What would happen if I overrode his tantrums? Would he run off to live with his father, leaving me unloved and alone? I would never be able to bear that.

It didn't occur to me that my son's challenges were his way of asking me to stop being so wishy-washy, to set limits, to please be someone of strength whom he could look to for guidance. My concern was to appease him to make him think I was wonderful—pretty, popular, a pal, a good guy. None of those were of any use to him; in fact, they confused and harmed him. He needed someone to give him values, to expect the best of him, to apply sanctions when he misbehaved. I had been a mother for twelve years, and I still had no concept of a mother's role. And at that time I was feeling too needy myself to attempt to learn the role.

During the early months after the separation, as I tried to cope with problems I felt unequal to, my intention was not to take care of another person, but to meet someone who would take care of me. And who would that person be? Why, a new man, of course.

I imagined a kind, loving person who would come into my life and transform it (I ignored the fact that in all my forty-six years I had never been even remotely involved with such a paragon of perfection). He would be warm and understanding, a male "authority figure" for my son. I envisioned the three of us on family outings, then pictured the man and myself walking along a sparkling, sun-drenched beach, hand in hand. We would have easy conversations, mutual interests, a terrific sex life, and, most important, we'd share financial burdens.

One spring day, as I walked in Central Park inhaling the

intoxicating fragrances of the pink and white, blossom-filled trees, I saw a young man and woman exchange a long, passionate kiss. My knees went weak with desire. Although my intellect told me that romance is transitory, soon giving way to the realities of two conflicting personalities, I still longed fervently to believe in the old "happily ever after."

So in May, when I started seeing Stuart, I unquestioningly cast him in the role of dream man.

I hadn't been in the least impressed with Stuart when I first met him. We had talked at length at a party, and I had found him singularly uninteresting and vapid. Moreover, he had been with a woman with whom he appeared to be involved, so after that night I forgot about him.

He called me two weeks later. It was a Saturday evening, and I had just finished laboring over a short story that I was sure no one would ever want to buy. The anxiety over my work was coupled with a sense of abandonment—my son was in the country with his father and all my friends were busy. The night was before me. What would it be—a solitary movie, a long, lonely walk, or a good book in the quiet emptiness of my apartment? And then the phone rang. I was saved! I didn't have to spend a dateless Saturday night, after all.

Stuart suggested we have supper, and I said I was looking forward to this particular film—I think it was *Harold and Maude*—and would he like to come with me? Indeed he would; he'd come by for me in fifteen minutes. I hung up in a frenzy of excitement: no time to wash my hair, but I could slip into some better-fitting jeans and a more flattering sweater—e.g., *tighter* jeans and *tighter* sweater. As I dashed about the apartment, I forgot my initial evaluation of Stuart and began to fantasize the beginning of a perfect relationship. I even imagined a sexual attraction, although I could barely remember what he looked like.

The blue-jeaned, fortyish man, with the petulant mouth and the modish rimless eyeglasses, whom I greeted at my front door was having his own fantasies. We were two breathless creatures talking excitedly past one another, weaving dreams that had nothing to do with the reality of Stuart and Greta.

Reality, in fact, was the farthest thing from my mind on that sensually warm May evening. A few minutes later, striding along Broadway next to this tall, slim man, I let go of the fragmented woman trying to build her own life, to make her own decisions. Now I was whole again; I was part of a couple. I was a woman of some importance, to be envied, even emulated.

In the movies we touched hands; then his hand stroked the inside of my thigh, my hand stroked his; then his arm was around me, his fingers caressing my breast. It was like those high school dates when we necked in the balcony of the Fox Wilshire movie house in Los Angeles: the same warmth suffusing my whole body; the same tingling in all the right places; the movie I had so wanted to see a total blur. When the film ended, Stuart and I rushed back to my apartment and into my double bed where we made feverish love—not at all like the high school days. He stayed the night, and in the morning we repeated the night's ecstasies, which were followed by one of those homey Sunday morning breakfasts. I was delighted. I had managed to get myself back in the old familiar domestic scene in which I felt most comfortable. It gave me the illusion that I had incorporated Stuart into my household.

Now I confess that conversation with Stuart was less than stimulating. His favorite subject was himself and his acquisitions. In addition, he was so competitive—everything of his had to be better and more expensive than anyone else's, from his automobile, his house in the country, to his psychoanalyst. No matter. I would withhold judgment in order to feel that I was attached to someone.

"I'll call you tomorrow," Stuart told me as he regretfully took his leave. But there was no call tomorrow, or the next day, or the day after that. I went into a tailspin; I was humiliated, abandoned, worthless. All my accomplishments of the past months paled without this person I imagined to be my anchor. I could barely work, and each day that the phone didn't ring was another day of rock-bottom self-esteem to live through.

My rational side pointed out that the anguish had nothing to do with Stuart since I barely knew him, and what I did know wasn't too impressive. And why assume that he wasn't calling because of an inadequacy in me? He was behaving rudely. Perhaps this was his standard way of operating with everybody, and why did I want to have anything to do with such a thoughtless individual? My emotions were not to be swayed by my intellect. I continued to wait for the phone to ring (of course, I'd never pick the phone up on the first ring; I'd let it ring two or three times, and then I'd answer in my most casual voice), and to sink into a depression when the caller turned out to be a friend or my ex-husband wanting to speak to our son.

Stuart phoned at the end of the week and asked to see me. He didn't apologize for not calling the next day as he had promised, and I didn't bring up the subject. I was so overjoyed to hear his voice, to once again feel a whole person, that I didn't dare make waves.

It was not one of your better relationships. (Why should this one be different from all others?) Stuart followed his pattern of saying he'd call the next day and then phoning a week or two later, while I followed my routine of going from elation to devastation. Our dates were never planned by Stuart. He'd call and ask if we could get together that evening, and if it was a night my son was visiting his father or a friend, I'd say yes. Most often we'd immediately make love, and afterwards I'd cook supper—and do the dishes. You're a fool, was the opinion of my rational self. My romantic, needy self turned a deaf ear.

Once I took the initiative and called Stuart to suggest we get together since I was free that night. His tone was gently reproving: "I like you," he told me, "but I can't be pressured. I have too many other pressures" (referring to a wife from whom he was separated, the woman he'd been with at the party whom he treated much as he treated me, and two children he saw about every two months). "I'll call you when I'm ready." I was properly vanquished.

During my saner moments, I tried to understand why I was getting so emotionally worked up over a man I barely knew and didn't much like. If I could tie my relationship with Stuart to past relationships, perhaps I'd be able to see it for what it was, to take away its power to hurt me so. I struggled to remember details about my parents and found they were vague. My father had always been remote and busy with work—that fit with Stuart. But what about my mother? She had been anxious and frightened, filled with presentiments of danger for herself and her family. My father, sister, and I had laughed at her fears, yet we had tried to assuage them. She had been the focus of our lives. But hadn't she always been kind to me? How did she fit in with my current pain? There was so much that was blurred.

The pain culminated at the funeral of a thirty-nine-year-old friend who had suffered from leukemia for a year. His illness had been especially difficult for those close to him because he had never acknowledged he was dying, and his family had decreed we must not tell him. Visits to the hospital had been strained with pretense as we listened to him speak gaily of future plans while we saw the unspoken terror in his eyes. There had been no opportunity to say good-bye.

Now, in the austere, airless chapel, I felt myself gagging on my friend's unresolved life and on my own crippling fears. Later, on the way to the cemetery—wedged between two people, the heat of the back seat stifling, small talk going on around me—the terrors were even more intense, pressing on my chest, cutting off my air, causing me to breathe in short, shallow gasps.

The cemetery was for rich people: sloping green hills, blossoming rhododendron, ornate marble headstones, and massive mausoleums. I wanted to sit down on the green grass with my head against the cool marble of a headstone—born 1872, it said. Perhaps, surrounded by this quiet, this peace, I might find the answers that would alleviate my pain. But there was no time for lingering. My friend's coffin, with its pretend-grass cover, was quickly lowered into the ground next to his father—also dead at age thirty-nine—and then we were off to the oppressiveness of our waiting automobiles.

Back in the city, alone in the clammy, air-conditioned apartment, I sat in the rocking chair in my living room and rocked back and forth, frantically trying to dislodge the lump that seemed to be stuck in my chest and throat. I had no one, I thought; again my son had abandoned me, off for a weekend with friends. I remembered my mother's funeral a year ago in the dazzling, sunlit chapel in West Los Angeles, with all of us wearing brightly colored clothes, my father in shock, and I acting like a hostess at a cocktail party rather than one of the bereaved. "Sit down," everyone admonished. "You shouldn't greet people. We'll come to you." But I wasn't comfortable having people come to me.

My mother had died suddenly of a heart attack, and by the time I got to Los Angeles, she was laid out neatly in a casket: a small woman with prominent cheekbones, a sharp nose, and a thin mouth that turned down at the corners— was it from bitterness? Disappointment? She had been all alone when death came, had been taking a bath. Had she been afraid? Did she call out when the first pain came? Did her anxious, pale-hazel eyes grow wide with fear when no one heared her voice? Was she conscious as she slowly slid beneath the water? I would never know.

I began to cry, huge, wrenching sobs, all the while aware

that no one in the world could hear me because I was sealed up in my air-conditioned room. I wanted my mother to be with me now, to rock away the miseries as she used to rock the "imps" away when I was naughty as a child. No! That was wrong! She never rocked them away. She rocked them in deeper. She couldn't tolerate my moods or my needs. They had to be banished. Only *she* could have problems and anxieties. *My* "imps" (such a demeaning word), my furies, had to be suppressed, to be stuffed back into me; and now they were surfacing. Except they were stuck in my throat and I couldn't spit them out and I didn't want to push them down anymore.

And at that moment it was as if a tiny piece of a complicated puzzle fell into place, and the torment I had been experiencing for weeks, and with such intensity during that day, began to subside. The crying stopped. I became calmer. The huge weight inside me began to dissolve. It occurred to me that all the men I'd been close to, including Stuart, were filled with problems and anxieties—"pressures," Stuart called them—and like my mother none had time or thought for me; their need was to have me available for comforting or company. Thinking my life depended on them, I had done all I could to comply.

Except I didn't need Stuart as I had needed my mother when I was a child. I could survive very well without him, just as I was surviving very well without my husband.

A week later Stuart called. "Hi," he said cheerily. "Remember me?"

"No," I replied quietly. "I don't." And I hung up.

Workshop II

Before we start the session, I mention to the group that on the way to the workshop I stopped at an elegant Italian restaurant for some pasta and wine. The food was delicious, the ambience terrific. I give it three stars and suggest they try it sometime.

Julia, the forty-six-year-old widow who is again dressed in conservative beiges and browns, looks at me with surprise. "You went to a restaurant alone?"

"Yes."

"Didn't you feel uncomfortable all by yourself?"

I reply that I didn't, that I found it very pleasant to sit quietly by myself after the tensions of a meeting I'd just come from.

"Didn't you have a feeling people were looking at you pityingly because you were all alone?" She emphasizes the word "alone."

"No. I don't think too many people paid any attention to me beyond a cursory look. There were two couples at the table next to me; they smiled as I sat down, and that was all."

Laura stares at me; her eyes are like dark brown half-dollars. I remind myself that she's the one who is miserable with her job and boyfriend, and is very dependent on her mother. She tells the group she's never in her life been to a restaurant alone. "I'd be terrified," she adds.

"Not even to a coffee shop?" plump, pretty Ann asks— she's in public relations, I mentally note; has a large network of friends.

Laura responds: "Oh, sure. I've gone to a coffee shop

44

alone a few times, but I don't even like to do that. I could never go to a fancy place." Her long fingers rake her jet-black frizz.

Elaine, our bejeweled married woman whose husband won't go places with her, remarks that she'd be very nervous at a nice restaurant without another person.

I ask if all the women feel that way. There are affirmative nods from Julia, Elaine, Laura, and blond, blue-eyed Susan. Ann and trim, slim, twenty-four-year-old Connie—a department store sportswear buyer—have different feelings. Connie claims she wouldn't be nervous, but she hasn't ever tried an expensive place alone, mainly because she can't afford it. Ann says she also has no fears, but prefers having company when she eats.

Julia wonders why anybody would want to eat alone.

I say that there are times when I find it luxurious to sit in beautiful surroundings, eating delicious food and drinking good wine, with no obligation to make conversation or to listen to someone else's conversation. "On the other hand," I continue, "there have been times in the past when my self-esteem was so low that I would have died rather than be seen alone in a restaurant. You do have to feel good about yourself."

"Do you go to movies alone?" Susan inquires.

I say that I do, and to plays and concerts. Ann and Connie also have gone to plays and movies alone: "Only to matinees, though," Connie adds.

Laura appears stunned. "I won't go anywhere without another person," she reveals. "Just last week there was a party in my neighborhood to meet some political candidates. I wanted to go, but I couldn't get anyone to go with me. So I stayed home."

"That happens to me all the time," Julia confides.

I tell her that's why I think it's important to be able to pick up and go places by herself. "You miss out on so much if you can't budge without a companion."

"Except most things are no fun when you do them alone. They're much better when they're shared," Julia opines.

Ann agrees with her.

"There are times when I want to be with another person," Connie says, "but there are other times when doing something alone can be fantastic. For instance, I really dig going to art galleries all by myself. I don't want to hear what anyone else has to say about the paintings. I just want to form my own opinions."

I mention that in one of her books Anne Morrow Lindbergh describes the pleasures of going to a concert alone. It's easier to concentrate on the music, she says. You're not distracted by the person beside you. You don't have to make conversation at intermission.

"It's so embarrassing to be alone when everyone else is in couples," Laura persists. "You just know people are looking at you, feeling sorry for you."

I remark that people will think their own thoughts for their own reasons, no matter what we do. The most important thing is how you feel about yourself: "Who knows, maybe some of the people at the restaurant tonight felt sorry for me—a poor woman eating all by herself. And there I was, having a wonderful time. You can't worry about other people."

Julia asks how one can begin to feel comfortable doing things alone, and I advise starting out with something she wants to do very much. Then I suggest she not put any great demands on herself: "If it's a party, go with the understanding that you can leave if you're not having a good time. Should you decide to eat out alone, just order something simple the first time—like my pasta and wine. If that's easy for you, you can get fancier the second time. The main thing to remember is that this is not an endurance test. You only want to open up more options, to make your life freer, more fun. So don't go into anything with gritted teeth and a do-or-die attitude. If you're not having fun, check out. Maybe you'll have better luck next time."

Ann advises avoiding Saturday night movies the first time Julia goes alone: "Being surrounded by couples can be a real downer if you're feeling at all vulnerable."

My final piece of advice is to keep her expectations realistic: "Go with a relaxed attitude. Take things for what they are, not for what you think they should be. You'll get much more pleasure that way. If your expectations aren't in the clouds, you won't continually fall to earth with a thud."

My last statement leads me to a topic we had touched on last week—how our unreal expectations of a relationship can prevent us from enjoying the reality of a relationship. I hark back to our discussion of our survival pattern, which makes us repeat dumb things, and add to that the fact that one of the main things we look for, as we try to assure our continued survival, is a "perfect parent."

I see six puzzled faces. "I don't get it," Laura comments.

I explain: "As children, we see our parents as perfect; as people who know all the answers; as strong adults who will make our lives joyous and happy forever. As we get older, we become aware that these parents have very few answers. We see their weaknesses and realize that, instead of giving us unending happiness, they're saddling us with all kinds of troubles. Since we feel we need strength from someone, we begin, unconsciously, to look for substitute perfect parents. And we look for them in our important close relationships.

"What very often happens is that when we meet someone new—a new man especially—we don't see him as he is. He's a faceless form on which we put our expectations, our fantasies. We think of him as someone who will share *everything* with us; who will be an extension of us; who will like what we like, breathe when we breathe. In the beginning, while we're all excited and keyed up, we can maintain the fantasy. But as we know the person better and are forced to look at him as he actually is, we have difficulty. We become very upset because he isn't behaving as we think he should. The truth is, he's behaving as he always has, only we don't want to know that. The more he exerts himself as a separate, flawed person, the more angry we get, or the more we try to push him into our fantasy mold. Even worse, the more rejected we feel."

Connie tells us she can respond to that. Just recently she and a man went to the ballet—at her suggestion. "When we got out I was floating, and he told me he hated it. My heart sank. I got so depressed. He hadn't shared my wonderful feelings. He had betrayed me and ruined the whole evening. But now I have to confess something," Connie goes on. "He had told me before we got the tickets that he didn't like ballet, and I hadn't paid any attention. I kept assuming because I liked it, he'd like it."

I tell her she has given us a perfect example of what I've been talking about. If she had listened to the man, she would have known how he felt, and she might have decided to go to the ballet with someone else. Or she and the man could have done something they both enjoyed. Or, if she had insisted on going with him, at least she would have been prepared for his response, and she wouldn't have been so depressed.

"Isn't that wild?" Connie muses. "What you're saying makes a lot of sense, and I never thought of it that way."

"I know," I answer. "A few years ago I never did, either."

Elaine wonders if what we're talking about applies to her and her husband. I reply that it does, that part of her recent unhappiness comes from her not having looked at her husband realistically along the way.

"He *did* go places with me for a long time, even though he didn't much want to," Elaine argues. "I kept thinking eventually he'd want to do more. But it worked out just the reverse."

I say: "If you had taken a clear look at him, you would have understood that if he disliked socializing for so many years, and always did it grudgingly, it was pretty unlikely he was suddenly going to turn into a social butterfly. That kind of transformation only happens in the movies or television."

Julia confides that she thinks she's probably caught up in looking for the perfect mate. "My marriage was so perfect," she maintains, "and I keep trying to duplicate it. Then I'm always furious when the men don't live up to my standards. But how can I give up looking for the best? I'm used to the best."

I remark that I don't know what her marriage was like, but I can't imagine that it didn't have its imperfections. She doesn't respond, and I remind myself that few widows will admit that their deceased husbands were less than perfect. It's something I can't dispute. But I do tell her that, even if her marriage was absolute heaven on earth, she can't expect other men to be replicas of her husband. She's going to have to look at each person as an individual.

"Men don't give enough anymore," Julia complains. "One man I've been going out with insists on being with his kids on weekends, instead of with me. I want to see him weekends. He owes me that."

"So tell him," counsels Laura.

"I do tell him," Julia replies angrily. "I tell him I get lonely on weekends. I want to be with him. He doesn't have to see his kids every weekend. But he won't see it my way."

From Laura: "Then he's a bastard."

I interrupt: "He's not a bastard. He has responsibilities that conflict with what Julia wants. He has his own problems. He's not put on this earth to keep Julia from being lonely. Julia, you'll do yourself a big favor, and you'll be a lot less angry, if you can come to terms with that."

"How the hell am I supposed to come to terms with that? I'm miserable on weekends when I'm alone." She certainly isn't the soft-spoken woman of last week.

I remind her of what I said in the first session—that she has to begin fashioning a life of her own, to establish interests that she can pursue so that she's not always dependent on someone else to shape her existence. That way she won't demand such perfection; she'll be able to enjoy this man for whatever he has to offer. She won't be so furious with him because he isn't somebody he can't possibly be. It's like Connie's friend; he doesn't enjoy ballet. She can spend her life schlepping him to dance concerts, trying to increase his appreciation, or she can leave him alone and share other things with him. It takes a lot of wear and tear out of a relationship.

"It scares me," Julia confides. "Maybe if I look at this man as he really is, I'll decide I don't like him at all. Then if I stop seeing him, I'll be alone."

"But you're alone anyhow," Connie volunteers. "What Greta's saying is that the sooner we confront that, the sooner we'll do something constructive about it. We'll stop living in this big fantasy world."

Julia doesn't answer.

Elaine mentions that she knows women with perfect marriages, and why shouldn't we all be entitled to the same thing?

"I knew a lot of people with perfect marriages, too," Ann remarks, gesturing with round, smooth arms. "Unfortunately, they all got divorced." Everyone laughs except Elaine.

"Who knows what really goes on between people?" I add. "Just because something looks perfect doesn't mean it is. Anyhow, it doesn't do any good to focus on what others have. All we can do is look, with unclouded vision, at what we have and then decide how we want to handle it."

When we've exhausted the subject for the evening, Susan
tells us she had some interesting insights as a result of last
week's discussion on how we repeat dumb behavior. "I saw
how I play the cute little girl in order to get people to do
things for me. What happened was that my boss had given
me some work to do that I wasn't able to finish. So I went
to his office, and I opened my blue eyes wide and looked
young and helpless and said, 'You don't *really* need those
papers today, do you?' And he laughed and said, 'You didn't
finish them, huh?' I gave him my sheepish, aren't-I-awful
look. He laughed again. 'Okay,' he said. 'Don't worry. I'll
get Jackie to do them.'

"I walked out of his office feeling pretty smart, and then
I remembered what we had talked about—how I always
get people to do things for me—and I thought, Boy! That's
what I just did. I acted like a little girl and I'm thirty years
old. And then I thought about doing things automatically,
not knowing you're doing them, and I could see that was
true for me. I was conning my boss just like I used to con
my mother into letting me stay home when I didn't feel
like going to school, and just like I used to con my teachers
into giving me an extension on a paper or a retest on an
exam I hadn't done well on." She giggles and tosses her
long, blond hair. "The truth is, the act usually works to my
advantage."

I ask her what the advantage is, and she replies that she
almost always gets what she wants.

"But look at the price you pay," I argue. "You've made
yourself into such a helpless child that you're afraid to do
the least little thing. It would be more to your advantage
to show yourself that you can get the work done like an
adult, rather than getting out of it like a little kid."

Her voice is flat when she answers: "I guess you're right."
I'm not at all sure she means it.

"I did do one thing," Susan continues. She now sounds

like a little girl who wants to please the teacher. "Remember, I said my firm would send me to school so I'd be in a better position for promotion? And remember I said I kept avoiding filling out the application? Well, I got the application for the school and I started to fill it out." She puts on her sheepish, aren't-I-awful face. "But I didn't quite finish filling it out. I couldn't decide what I wanted to take. I thought I'd talk it over with my boyfriend."

Connie bursts out: "Susan, you are too much! You're old enough to fill out your own application. I do things like that all the time, and I'm six years younger than you are."

I echo Connie's sentiments and say to Susan that she's got to start taking some intiative somewhere, and the school application is as good a place to start as any. She doesn't need her boyfriend to tell her what to take; she can decide for herself.

"You can't go on acting like a ten-year-old forever," I add. "It's really harmful. Right now, some folks find it cute and they laugh—they have their own reasons for playing your game—but in ten or fifteen years nobody will laugh. Instead, you'll be fired for incompetence. Moreover, all that cutesy behavior will look ridiculous on a forty-year-old woman. So do the application. It's a minimal bit of responsibility, and you can certainly handle it. Let yourself know that you can take care of yourself."

Susan nods and looks contrite. She's still the little girl. Well, I think, at least she's not smiling vacantly and batting her eyelashes at me. A small step forward.

Julia mentions that she noticed something about *herself* this past week. She speaks slowly, reflectively. She's lost the anger of a few minutes ago. She says that she became aware that she wants her son and daughter, especially her daughter who is the older, to take care of her in the same way her husband did.

Elaine wonders what she means.

Julia tells her that she often goes to her son and daughter

for advice and for help in fixing things. She expects them
to cheer her up when she's depressed, to be available to
go places with her when she's at loose ends. "The way Phil,
my husband, always was. Last week I was very upset because my daughter didn't call and send flowers on the date
of my wedding anniversary. Phil always sent yellow roses
on our anniversary, and Jody, my daughter, has been doing
it since he died. This year she forgot. She felt awful when
I reminded her, but I couldn't forgive her. I felt she should
have remembered. Then my son got mad at me. He said
I expect too much of them, that there's no reason Jody
should send me flowers each year just because Phil did. He
said I'm always asking him to do things I could do myself,
and I've got to stop expecting them to jump every time I
call." She shrugs. "I don't know. Maybe he's right. I feel
I need them. I can't find a man to take care of me, so I
have to lean on them." She looks at me and smiles faintly.
"You think I shouldn't lean on any of them. Right?"

I smile back. "Right."

"Why shouldn't she?" Elaine bursts out indignantly. "Why
shouldn't our children think about us after all the years
we've given them? My daughter owes me something. But
she doesn't think so. She tells me it's not her fault that I
gave up things for her. She says she can't spend her life
making that up to me, that she has her own life, and right
now it happens to be with her husband in New Mexico.
It's not right."

I tell her I understand her feelings because for a long
time I had the same expectations of my son. Here I'd been
this "giving, loving mother," and he wasn't reciprocating.
I point out that it's wanting the perfect parent again—we'll
take care of our children and in exchange they'll never
forsake us; they'll keep us free from loneliness and anxiety
forever. That's an unfair and unreal request to make of
them.

"Why is it?" Elaine questions me angrily, jabbing the air

with diamond-ringed fingers. "We did plenty for them. Why shouldn't they do for us?"

I reply: "They don't owe us anything. What we did for them was not for them but for ourselves. We behaved in certain ways because that's how we chose to behave. Let's not kid ourselves that we made all kinds of sacrifices. We had children because we wanted to; we raised them in certain ways because we wanted to. They don't owe us any debt of gratitude for that."

"I think they do."

Ann interrupts to suggest that Elaine and Julia would do better to form a network of women friends, rather than depending on children and men.

Julia asks how that works.

"My friends and I help each other," Ann explains. "We're available for each other—the way you'd like this man to be, or your kids to be. If I'm having a hard time, I'll call one of my woman friends, and she'll come over and see me through the depression or whatever it is I'm going through. I'll do the same for her. There's a group of us. If one can't come, you call someone else. It's not just for trouble, of course. You share good things as well."

From Elaine: "Where do you find all the friends?"

Ann replies that you have to work at it: "You have to cultivate women who can be warm, nourishing, supporting friends. For instance, if I meet someone who I think could be a good friend, I go out of my way to get to know her. I let her know that I'm available, that I'll be there for her. I introduce her to my other friends. It doesn't just happen quickly. It takes a long time to establish a close relationship with someone."

Laura asks me if I have such a network of friends, and I answer that I have many friends who are terrific and who can be helpful—just as I'm helpful to them. But I don't have a network, as Ann describes. When it comes to dealing with emotional problems, I prefer to work things out alone.

"What do you do, though, when you get anxious and you can't stand being alone, when you just need someone there to keep you from climbing the walls? I go crazy when I get like that. I call practically everyone I know."

The subject of anxiety produces a strong response in all the women. Each relates her own method for coping with the dread emotion. Connie says she tries to ignore it: "I go about my business even though I'm feeling awful; after a few hours, or a few days, the anxiety goes away. But it always comes back."

Ann calls a friend to help her through the pain; Susan turns to her boyfriend. Elaine makes herself busy in the kitchen: "I cook and bake up a storm." Julia says she clutches like mad at her children or a current lover—if he's available.

I tell them that I used to do all the things they've mentioned, but through my psychotherapy I've learned to confront the anxiety and to try to understand the reasons for it. "Now that I've become proficient in working through my feelings," I add, "I find that I don't get anxious very often, and when I do it's not nearly as intense as it used to be."

At their request, I explain the method: "The first step is to stop your old methods—the running around, the frantic phone calls, etc. I force myself to sit down. Then I ask myself questions; I do it on paper or I talk out loud, but you can do it in your head. Then I try to answer the questions.

"Some of the questions are: What exactly am I feeling? Does the feeling remind me of feelings I had as a child? When? Where? With whom? Is it logical to be as anxious now as I was then? What was going on in the past situation that frightened me so? What is going on now that is frightening? Aren't things quite different now than they were in the past? How? Haven't I always survived similar anxiety-provoking experiences? So why should I be so terrorized now? What's the worst thing that could happen in this situation? Could I live through the worst? If I can live through the worst, what is there to be afraid of?"

I point out that the purpose of the question-and-answer technique is to bring the anxiety down to size, to take it out of that vague, inexplicable-terror category. When you face the irrationality of your feelings—and anxiety is almost always irrational—you feel much more in control and a lot less frightened. "At first the process takes time," I warn them. "When you're agitated, just sitting down quietly is a struggle, especially when your automatic response is to fly off in a million directions. But once you get the hang of it, you can go through the process fairly quickly." I suggest they all try it and see for themselves. I promise to bring in a typed list of the questions next week.

Connie brings up the final topic of the evening. It concerns her job. She explains that she's been a buyer for her department for a year and a half. The woman who hired her liked her and gave her a great deal of freedom and encouragement. Three months ago her boss took a job in another city. She was replaced by a woman who for some reason can't stand Connie.

"I don't know why," she says. "I've knocked myself out to please her. I know I'm good at what I do, yet I get nothing but criticism. It's like she's looking to find fault."

"Why not talk to her?" Ann suggests, her round face full of concern. "Maybe she doesn't realize how she's acting toward you."

"She realizes," Connie responds grimly.

"Maybe she feels threatened by you," Ann continues. "You're very good-looking, you're young and smart."

"What can I do about that?"

I say to Connie that there's probably no way of understanding her boss's feelings toward her, and even if there were a way, it's unlikely she'd be able to do much about them. I point out that she's done the best she can with no results. Now she's going to have to think about what *she* wants to do. Since she can't alleviate the situation, she may have to ask to be changed to another department, or, if worse comes to worst, look for another job.

"That infuriates me," Connie answers. "Why should that bitch force me out?"

"Do you see any other way?"

With resignation: "No. I just hate giving her the satisfaction of winning."

I caution against getting caught up in her boss's game. She should concentrate on her own needs. "There was a woman in one of my other workshops," I relate, "who was inexplicably hated by her boss as you are. He told her she was incompetent, although she had always been praised for her competence. She was so enraged that she refused to quit, refused to ask for a change of department. Her big goal was to make him admit that she was competent. Like you, she knocked herself out to do well, and he fired her anyway. Once she was out of a job, she began to doubt herself, to believe that she might really be incompetent. She became nervous about looking for another job. It took her a long time to find something. Had she made some decisions while still working, I'm sure it would have been a different story."

Connie admits that what I'm saying sounds right, but she can't help wanting to know the boss's reason for not liking her. It drives her crazy not being able to understand what's going on.

"She may not know herself," I answer. "One of the things I've learned about people is that they don't always operate in nice, logical, rational ways. Your boss has her own automatic behavior pattern. Worry about yourself, not about her."

Laura interrupts to tell us that she can relate to what we're talking about: "I always figure that if I'm doing my part, I should be patted on the back. But it never works that way, especially with my boyfriend. I do everything his way, and he treats me like dirt. He'll disappear for days, not call me or anything; then he'll turn up and get mad if I ask for an explanation. Sometimes he'll go into a sulk for no reason. I try to understand him, to get him to tell me what's bothering him, but he won't. What I'm getting from the discussion tonight is that he may not know himself what's bothering him."

I answer that he may very well not.

"So," Laura asks slowly, "I could be nice and understanding forever, and there's no way he'll ever be able to tell me what's going on?"

I say: "That's right. Like Connie, you have to stop focusing on the other person and start thinking about yourself. Instead of worrying about his problems, ask yourself why you continue in such a depressing relationship. What are you getting out of it? How do you perpetuate it? How does it resemble past relationships? What do you want to do about it?"

"I keep thinking he's better than nothing. I'm not getting any younger, and it's hard to find someone. And I keep thinking he'll change. But what you're saying makes me feel maybe he won't." Laura's exotic features suddenly become dark and remote. "I guess I don't want to talk about it anymore." In her usual fashion, she has unequivocally closed the subject.

The other women return their attention to Connie. They urge her to take steps on her own behalf before it's too late. Connie agrees to think about it, and the session is over. The women again go off to the coffee shop, and I wend my way up Madison Avenue.

It's very cold tonight so I turn up the collar of my coat and thrust my hands deep in my pockets. I think about the women: the way Laura abruptly retreats when a subject gets uncomfortable; how Ann has advice for everyone else but doesn't reveal much about herself. I wonder if Julia will ever allow herself to see the imperfections of her marriage; maybe never. Will Connie do something about her job? I have a feeling she will. I think about Susan's cutesy behavior. She gets a lot of feedback from it, and she's not going to let go of it too easily. But then, is there anyone who lets go of old habits easily? Elaine was angry with me tonight because I told her that her daughter didn't owe her any debt of gratitude. She didn't want to hear that. She probably doesn't even believe me. I wonder if Ann might be a little angry, too; I'm never very sympathetic about her network of friends.

I want the women to like me, to think well of me. The thought brings back a statement made by my therapist. I had expressed concern about members of another workshop not liking me, and she had observed that I wasn't there to be liked. "You're there to do a job. If you let your ego get in the way of leading the workshop, you won't be able to do your job effectively."

She was right. When I worry about making an impression, about being a popular workshop leader, I don't concentrate as well on the task at hand. Still, being popular has always been such a strong goal for me that it's hard not to pursue it automatically. I'll have to keep checking myself.

An icy blast of wind reminds me how cold it is. I quicken my pace, and in fifteen minutes I'm home.

Chapter III

My son took an ounce of milk from my breasts this morning. That was the most wonderful thing in the whole world.
—From my journal, December 15, 1961

Just screamed at my son for trying to stop me from writing. The lid is coming off. My head is bursting. I can't be his mother. I can't exist with one other person around. I'll explode. I do explode. I want to walk out the door and never come back. I think it's all a crock of shit—motherhood, wife, life.
—From my journal, October 6, 1965

I have always delighted in recalling my good-bye to Stuart. What a curtain line it would make. How wonderful to report that after such a smashing finis to a rotten romance (I use the term "romance" loosely) I was free at last of the old way, ready to embrace a "warm, loving relationship."

Unlike the theater, life rarely works that way. Most often, one simply rings down the curtain on one scene and then unconsciously proceeds to set the stage for another quite like it. And so, even as I hung up the phone after my rejection of Stuart, I was concentrating on finding someone else with whom I could assume my familiar role. For the moment, there was no one new, at least no adult. But there was always my son. In many ways, the scene we played together day in and day out was not so different from the

scene I had enacted for seventeen years with his father,
and for a couple of months with Stuart.

I was beginning to discover how frightened I was of my
son. With great effort, I was trying to learn how to be the
head of the house while still attempting to placate my child
at all costs. He, like the men I had known, would keep
me from feeling adrift, undefined. I couldn't take any
chances of incurring his displeasure. Therefore, I vacillated
continually. I'd set down rules, and when they were disregarded I'd be too afraid of losing him to apply sanctions.
When I did manage to have some small effect on my son's
behavior, I'd breathe a sigh of relief. Everything was
solved. I didn't have to worry anymore. He was a new
person. When a day later he was up to his old tricks again,
I'd be caught unawares, devastated by what I considered
a betrayal. I so wanted to believe in miracles.

I continued to play my survival role—the uncomplaining,
misunderstood servant. I was always humbly there to mop
up the results of my son's defiance. I have painful memories
of my weeping self down on my knees, picking up pieces
of broken plate, trying, without success, to conceal gouged
holes in walls and floors, mending chairs that were thrown
or slammed in a fit of temper. And as I sobbed, swept,
patched, and fingered with despair a particularly loved
object that was shattered, I had the frightening perception
that the behavior I had devised for survival was, in fact,
the very thing that was slowly and painfully destroying me.

Still, it was the only game I knew, and I had taught my
son to play it like a master. He wasn't going to stop out of
the goodness of his heart; he thought it was *his* survival kit.
I was the one who would have to put an end to the game.
And that could only be accomplished by my taking on a
new role. But the thought of standing tall and making my
demands stick seemed so hard, so terribly wearying. I
wanted to command respect, to say in a sure, strong voice:
"This is the way it has to be"; at least I thought I did. But

why did my whole body become like jelly at the mere idea?

There was another factor that made my attempts to gain some bit of control doubly hard. I was convinced that I had the power to damage this frail creature entrusted into my care. (Frail, indeed! He weighed almost as much as I and in a year would be able to arm-wrestle me to the ground in a matter of seconds.) Therefore, if he expressed all kinds of irrational fears and made the most outrageous demands, I would turn myself inside out in order to accommodate him. He in turn had my number down pat, and he let me know that if he was having troubles it was all my fault. And I'd better make things right.

Of course it was my fault. What did he want me to do? I'd do anything I could.

I never stopped to evaluate what was going on. I didn't ask myself what was best for me and what was best for him. I had not been taught to take the time to think and as yet hadn't taught myself. My primary goal, learned at the parental knee, was to come up with answers and solutions as quickly as possible. Neither of my parents had been able to tolerate a moment's anxiety, so there had been the constant necessity to obliterate all problems immediately, even if it meant going against my own feelings and needs.

Such was the case during a trip I took with my parents to Lake Tahoe when I was fourteen. My father had rented a house for the three of us, sight unseen—my younger sister had been left at home with my grandfather, despite the fact that she would celebrate her tenth birthday while we were away, something for which she never quite forgave my parents. After a long drive, we reached a beautiful, spacious house at the water's edge. Every window of its eight rooms looked out on the lake. The living room and master bedroom had fireplaces. Tall French doors in the dining room opened onto a clean, white, sandy beach. It was a fantastic house. Since we had always lived in two-family duplexes, I was ecstatic at the prospect of a place all our own.

But to my father's and my amazement, the sight of such grandeur distressed my mother beyond belief. Tearfully and hysterically, she went from room to room crying, "It's too big! It's too big!" She walked through one of the bathrooms, hitting out blindly at the shower curtain like a terror-stricken child, repeating in a whining voice that it was too much for her to cope with, that she couldn't be expected to handle such an enormous place. "Too big for just the three of us," she wailed.

There was no talk that day of my mother's irrationality. My father didn't point out that we were there only for a week's vacation and no one expected her to run the house in a grand fashion. He didn't suggest that she'd be more at home after living in the house for a day. It was not argued that our duplex at home consisted of seven rooms, almost the same number as this wonderful lake house.

What happened was that we got back into the car, drove some fifteen minutes until we found a two-room cabin, and settled in. There was no view from any of the tiny windows, and we had to drive to the lake. I was bitterly disappointed and confused, yet never thought to question my mother or reproach her. My fourteen-year-old's vague interpretation was that had I protested this inexplicable move, I would be opening up a Pandora's box of horrors that might drive my mother over the brink and thus deprive me of her forever—something too frightening to contemplate, much less risk.

And now, thirty-one years later, I was going through the same routine with my twelve-year-old son, projecting onto him the precarious nervous system of my mother, imagining dark happenings if I allowed him to experience discomfort. Thus, if he waked me a dozen times during the night to say he was "scared," I jumped through hoops to take away his fears. When he revealed that he must rush to Alan's or

Charlie's or his father's on school nights because he was too anxious to stay home, I let him—I even paid for the cabs. When he claimed he didn't like what I was preparing for supper and had to have something different, I cooked something different.

It didn't occur to me to point out that he was old enough to handle his fears alone—that is, if he was really afraid—and that I had a right to a complete night's sleep. I never asserted, or perhaps only feebly, that nothing is ever resolved by rushing from place to place and I wanted him to stay put (since I was doing a bit of rushing myself in those days, I was not one to talk). I didn't tell him that if he must have special foods, he could jolly well prepare his own meals.

No! I was still performing in the old scene. The cast of characters had changed, but the action was the same. The worst part of it was that most of the time I didn't know I was doing it.

I did know, however, that change was imperative. But where to start? There was so much going on that it was dizzying. My therapist advised I begin by observing my son in order to see him as he really was. She commented that I treated him like a stick figure instead of a three-dimensional person. For example, I waited on him with the expectation that he would be grateful and would want to do things for me in return. That was unrealistic. That was not my son's way of responding. Yet I kept going through the same motions again and again, always furious and disappointed because he wasn't coming through in the "appropriate fashion." If I had taken the time to deal with him as a separate, special individual, I would be compelled to change my behavior and my expectations.

I started to watch him, to think about him. I saw that his pattern of responding to my "kindnesses" involved his demanding more—and more and more. Forget about thank you's. As for returning the favor, he didn't know the meaning of the phrase. I could see that part of his reaction had to do with inertia, but another part came from a genuine belief that he couldn't do very much, that he must always look to me.

I decided to try to break the pattern in one small area—the after-school snack. Because I worked at home, it had been my habit to stop work the minute my son came home from school in order to make him something to eat. It seems like a perfectly innocuous thing to have done, and in some situations it would have been fine. In our case, it was destructive to both of us for several reasons. Here was one small task my son could easily perform for himself and I was depriving him of it; bustling about the kitchen in the middle of the afternoon allowed me to play my indispensable-mother game—a game I was trying to end; jumping up from my work the minute my son walked in was telling him (and myself) that my work wasn't important, that it could easily be interrupted.

Although stopping such a ritual sounds like a one-afternoon operation, it actually took several months. It was a simple routine, but the emotions connected with it were far from simple; they were complicated and fraught with confusions, and it took some time to sort them out.

The first afternoon I refused to make the snack my son protested loudly. He banged on my office door and in an imperious voice told me that I wasn't doing anything important. The least I could do was make him a sandwich. Immediately I was assailed by doubts and anxiety. Why couldn't I do that small thing for him? I asked myself. It wouldn't really take that much time. But that's not the point, I countered. It's not the time you're concerned with. You're trying to show him that he can do for himself, that he shouldn't continually rely on you. I know that, but if he makes his own snack maybe it won't be nutritious; isn't it important he have wholesome, nutritious food? Answer: He won't die if he eats a piece of cake instead of a cheese sandwich.

My son's voice came through the door again: "Just this once, Mom. I've had such a hard day at school." He suddenly sounded piteous and weak. "Can't you do this for me just this once?"

Maybe he *is* overworked at school, I worried. Maybe he should have something nourishing after a long, hard day. Are you crazy? was my reply. He barely cracks a book. He does as little school work as he can legitimately get away with. Don't let him con you.

But I was determined to make a case for him. I told myself that I could easily stop what I was doing, that, in fact, it would be nice to get away from my desk for a few minutes. He did sound very tired. Seconds later, I was in the kitchen making the snack. And once again I became furious that instead of saying thanks to me, my son started pushing for a dozen other favors. Next time, I resolved, no giving in.

As I became stronger in my resolve, my son brought out stronger ammunition. He sure knew how to get to me: "You're not the nice mother you used to be. I don't like you anymore"—a knife right through my heart. "If you don't make me a snack, I won't eat anything at all"—he'll die of malnutrition, and everyone will blame me. Some days I'd stick to my guns, and on others I'd relent. I still hadn't made a firm commitment to a specific policy. And my son knew it. As long as I wavered the tiniest bit, he would be there to push his case.

But the months of trial and error and the ongoing interior arguments paid off. The wavering stopped. Ultimately, I knew beyond a doubt—and more important, *felt* beyond a doubt—that even if I was doing nothing of great consequence, even if I was just reading a book or sitting idly, it was absolutely necessary that my son make his own after-school snack. Here was one area where I didn't have to be at his beck and call.

I explained my reasoning to my son. It wasn't a punishment I was meting out, I told him. I was simply offering him a chance to use himself more, to see that he didn't need me so much. In addition, it was important that he and I take my work and my time more seriously. Neither of us should expect me to jump up at his every whim.

He wasn't buying any of it, but by then he knew he didn't have any choice. I was no longer pushable. It was either make his own snack or go without. He grumbled and complained for many weeks afterward, but he made his own snack.

With that small victory in my pocket, I felt courageous enough to look at my son's nightly dashing about. It had gotten to the point where he was always on the move. One night it was to a friend's; on another it would be an unscheduled visit to his father's. Often, on the night he was scheduled to visit his father, he'd go, stay for an hour, and then decide he had to go home. In the early months I had assumed the running around was due to the upheaval in our life, and he would soon tire of it. I had fervently hoped that I wouldn't have to go through the ordeal of setting down some rules. What good would it do, anyhow? He so rarely listened to me.

But as the months went by with no change of behavior, and as I began to look at my son as the person he was, I had to admit that he was not one to make rational life decisions. He was a twelve-year-old boy, not my perfect parent, and if anyone was going to make a decision on this issue it was going to have to be me. Okay, I told myself with little enthusiasm, I'll do something. But I had faint hope for success.

My initial attempts to deal with the problem were pathetic. Instead of telling my son what to do in no uncertain terms, I tried to cajole him into making a different choice.

"Don't you think you ought to stay home tonight?" I would query him in an anxious, small-girl voice.

"No."

"Don't you have homework? If you have homework, you really should stay home." (Almost pleading with him.)

"I'll get it done."

"You really don't get proper sleep when you run around like that. It's important you get enough sleep."

At one point, I resolved that the best thing to do was to wash my hands of the whole affair. "Go where you want," I told my son. "Do what you want. It's your problem, not mine."

He did exactly as I said.

Stand up to him, I counseled myself. Things are totally out of hand. You have a responsibility to stop him.

I'm afraid of him, I answered. I'm afraid of his violence. He'll tear the house apart if I oppose him.

It's true he has a violent temper, my rational side agreed, but he knows when to stop. He's broken small things, but nothing of great value. This is important enough to risk a few broken things.

I'm afraid he'll leave me if I oppose him. He'll go live with his father and never come back.

If he can't live with your rules, then let him go.

A shiver of fear: I couldn't bear that. I want him with me.

You've got to take chances. You've played it safe for too long, and it's not worked. It's not good this way. It's time to make your voice heard.

I knew it was time, and I was afraid. How awful to be afraid of your own child. But once you've begun to question, to look at new possibilities, fear is not a deterrent. You simply can no longer continue with the old ways. You have to go forward; you must try the alternatives.

I confronted my son on a Tuesday night as he was getting ready to go to a friend's house. With trembling knees and

aching temples, I went into his room and told him I wanted
to talk to him.

"Yeah? Whaddya want?"

"I've decided you've got to stop the running around on
school nights," I declared in the firmest tone I could muster.

"You told me I could go anywhere I wanted."

"I know I did, but I've changed my mind."

Outrage: "You can't do that. You promised."

Getting bolder: "Oh, yes, I can. I've thought it through
carefully, and I see that I made a mistake. It's not good for
you to run around as you've been doing. So just stop for a
minute and listen to what I've decided." He glared at me
and doubled his fists, but I went on. "On Sundays and
Wednesdays you go to your father's house as has been ar-
ranged. And you stay there; you don't come running home
at the least little provocation. On Monday, Tuesday, and
Thursday you stay home; on Friday and Saturday nights
you may stay over at anybody's house you choose. I see
you're getting ready to go out, but since tonight is Tuesday,
you will stay home."

"*Get out of my room!*" he roared. "*Get out before I kill
you!*"

I got out fast, and the door slammed after me. I heard
something crash against the wall, then the sound of breaking glass. A few minutes later there was pounding and curs-
ing. Then silence.

Feeling faint, I went into the living room and sat on the
couch and waited for my son to come out, suitcase in hand,
en route to his friend's house or to his father's. So be it.
I would live without him. Rivers of tears flowed down my
cheeks.

But my son didn't emerge from his room the rest of the
evening, except once to borrow my dictionary. He was doing his homework. The subject was closed. From that night
on, the rules were observed.

Incredible! He did what I told him to!

"He's been waiting twelve years for you to tell him what to do," my therapist remarked when I related the incident.

Twelve years! It made me cry. Such a long time for a child to wait.

Why cry? argued my rational self. Look on the bright side. At least he hasn't waited in vain.

Chapter IV

I am always bothered because people don't respond to situations when I want them to and the way I want them to. It's as though people shouldn't have lives and feelings of their own but should be wholly dependent on my whims. What a childish dream that is.

—From my journal, November 30, 1961

In July of 1974, my son went off to New Hampshire for two months of summer camp. The day after his departure, I went off to visit my friends, Ron and Sue Frankel. They had invited me to spend the Fourth of July weekend with them in their vacation house in Westhampton, Long Island.

It was to be my first weekend away since the separation, and I was terribly excited. Who knew what adventures lay in store for me now that I was temporarily free from my mothering chores? The combination of sand, sea, and blue sky would provide the perfect setting for a "fun-filled" holiday. And maybe—Oh, let it be so!—part of the fun would be an encounter with a congenial person of the opposite sex.

As it turned out, it wasn't an adventurous weekend, but it was "fun-filled." I swam and bicycled with the Frankels' two teen-aged daughters, Annie and Melissa, snorkeled with the couple next door, and talked endlessly with Ron and Sue. There was a great deal of cooking and eating and wine drinking—a welcome respite from articles to be written, bills to be paid, and emotional problems to work through. It was also a joy to be with an affectionate family after so many years of a tension-filled household.

71

Yet, with all the pleasures, there were moments of envy: Why couldn't I have a "happy marriage" with two warm, loving children? Did Sue know how blessed she was to be able to share with Ron, rather than going it alone? Look how kind and considerate they were to each other. Soon the Frankels were enveloped in a rosy glow: I saw them unencumbered with cares and conflicts of the real world; the children were always tanned and healthy, their skin free of adolescent acne; mother and daughters consistently spoke to one another in soft, modulated voices; no money worries or arguments disrupted my fantasy of their tranquil life.

The more I cast them in their exalted roles, the more I pitied poor Greta who had to fashion a life alone. Not fair! I cried to myself. Not fair! They have gotten so much with very little effort, and I have to work so hard for a bare existence.

But wait, countered my rational self, don't get all carried away. These are flesh-and-blood people who are just as much prey to the vicissitudes of living as you are. Didn't Ron tell you he is having great troubles in his business, that he's tremendously in debt? And look how nervous he is; it's difficult for him to sit still. He must always be doing something, fixing something. His nails are bitten to the quick. Does he appear to you like a man at peace?

And be honest. Although you like and respect Sue, would you want her life? Ron definitely rules the roost, albeit kindly, and that's the kind of relationship you're trying to get away from. And another thing; you don't know what goes on between Sue and Ron, and between the girls and their parents, when no one is around. And you don't know what goes on in their heads. All people have their private struggles and fears. The Frankels are no exception.

Last of all, pointed out my unrelenting rational self, even if their life is perfection itself, fretting and comparing will do you absolutely no good. What they have is theirs and what you have is yours, and there's nothing you can do

about it. You're going to have to make the best of the life
you have, and you may very well have to do it forever as a
woman alone.

Don't say that, pleaded my fantasizing self desperately.
I grew up in the forties, and all those songs and movies told
me how it should be. A woman has to have a man, and a
man can't be without a mate, they said, and everyone *always* lived happily ever after. Didn't Mr. Miniver come
back to Mrs. Miniver after she waited patiently so many
years? I still can't help believing in that. I still can't help
wanting that.

To which there was no reply. My rational self had turned
away in disgust.

On the Fourth of July the Frankels gave a huge clam-
bake. It was wonderfully festive, with guests coming from
several adjacent beach communities as well as from Westhampton. Through the afternoon and evening we all swam
in the clear bay waters in front of Ron and Sue's house and
gorged ourselves on lobster, clams, barbecued chicken, corn
on the cob, salad, homemade cornbread, etc., etc., etc. One
of the guests was a forty-eight-year-old widower whose tall,
angular frame, sharp, thin features, piercing gray eyes, and
flyaway gray-black hair gave him the appearance of a rather
large bird. His name was Andrew.

Andrew came to the party with a pretty, thirtyish, dark-
haired woman with whom he was spending the weekend.
I liked her a lot, thought he was somewhat affected, and
wondered what she saw in him. When we all went swim-
ming, Andrew appeared in a shiny brown bikini—the only
man in such an abbreviated swimsuit. I mentally noted,
with some distaste, that he was probably very vain about
his body, which I had to admit was in remarkable shape for
someone in his late forties.

I spoke to him briefly when we were out in the bay tread-
ing water—something about the warmth and the calm of the
bay and weren't we lucky to be in this gorgeous spot on

such a lovely day—and that was the extent of our contact. The rest of the time I talked to the various other guests, including Andrew's date, Michele. She worked in the stock market, and I listened with fascination as she described her job; a woman with an expertise in finance was something quite new to me. She further impressed me by revealing that she had recently purchased her beach house and was in the process of fixing it up. How extraordinary! A woman in her thirties capable of buying a house out of her own earnings. Would I ever make enough money to be able to do such a thing? It seemed terribly unlikely. I didn't even have enough to reupholster my couch and chair.

The party was over at midnight, and the following day I returned to New York. Back to reality.

Andrew phoned me two days later. At first I couldn't recall him, but as he refreshed my memory a picture of a very tall bird in a brown bikini came to mind. "Ah, yes," I said, surprised by his call. "Now I remember you. How are you?" My voice automatically took on the musical, enthusiastic tone reserved for "new man."

"Fine," he replied. "I wonder if you'd like to have dinner with me." He quickly added, "I do want you to know that Michele and I have broken up. Fourth of July was our last weekend together. So if you're not seeing anyone regularly, I'd love to take you to dinner."

Incredible, I mused. Finished with one, on to the next. "No, I'm not involved with anyone," I trilled, "and it would be lovely to see you."

"How about next Monday?"

"Wonderful." I came close to hitting high C before hanging up.

Dinner was not unpleasant, but then again it wasn't terribly pleasant, either. Andrew told me that he had been a widower for four years, had two grown sons—one in college, one married. He confessed that he still felt deeply the loss of his wife, whom he depicted as beautiful, brilliant,

and completely understanding—a tough act to follow, I
thought, suddenly feeling very mousy and average. He
talked at length about his work as the director of a small
private hospital, and I was impressed by his apparent confidence in his skills. Since I was having difficulty believing
in my own abilities and often found my tongue becoming
twisted when pushed to describe myself as a writer, I tended
to overvalue anyone else's expression of high self-esteem.
Deep in my heart I suspected I was a pretender, and it
would only be a matter of time before the world discovered
my fraud.

That evening there was no worry on that score. Andrew
was far more interested in keeping the conversation focused
on all aspects of his own life than on mine. And that included his various love affairs since the death of his wife.

My thoughts through dinner went something like this:
He's intelligent, obviously well read and knowledgeable
about music, but his gossiping about all his women is sleazy.
It's especially tactless of him to tell me about Michele,
whom I know. His values are so different from mine;
already he's told me that he only wears expensive suits, that
his home is furnished with elegant antiques, and that he
has a lot of "important" friends. I couldn't care less. I wish
we were more alike. Why can't he be someone who shares
my feelings? He does have a nice sense of humor, though,
and he really seems to like me, even if I'm not as spectacular
as his dead wife. I wonder what he sees in me.

After dinner we went back to my apartment and talked.
Andrew let me know that he was very attracted to me and
that he loved being with me. I immediately dismissed my
earlier objections. It was nice to have an attentive man in
my life. I thought of asking him to spend the night but
cautioned myself against the same mindless involvement I
had experienced with Stuart. This time I'll go slowly, I resolved. When it grew late, I suggested Andrew leave since
I had to get up early the next morning. He explained he'd

have to take a taxi home because he hadn't brought his car into the city. He lived in a posh suburb of New Jersey, just over the George Washington Bridge.

"Do you think I'll be able to get a cab?" he inquired in a worried voice. "This is a pretty rough neighborhood, isn't it? In these expensive clothes, I'm a perfect target for muggers."

Ah, come on, I wanted to say. This neighborhood couldn't be safer. I come home at all hours alone, and so do my neighbors. This is a crosstown street, and there are taxis going by constantly. Besides, you're six-feet-two, and you can take care of yourself. So stop acting like a baby.

Instead I said, "Oh, all right. You can spend the night," and watched a delighted smile spread across his big-bird face.

And with that inauspicious beginning, my relationship with Andrew was launched.

Through the next two months, I wove Andrew into the fabric of my life. He was *the* man, the person whose call I waited for, the subject of my fantasies of future happiness, the source of many of my disappointments. We saw each other once or twice a week; we went to dinner, to movies and plays and concerts, and even shared a weekend in Nantucket.

I was enjoying myself, but I was always dissatisfied. I wanted more. I felt I gave a tremendous amount to the relationship and received very little in return. I always looked great on our dates, was full of vitality and interesting conversation; I was warm and loving in bed; I was constantly ready to listen to Andrew's problems; I was generous with help and advice.

But Andrew didn't respond as I felt he should. He was remote, not always available, sometimes moody for no apparent reason, not affectionate in the ways I craved.

I suggested to myself that I wasn't exactly crazy about Andrew, yet I was expecting him to be head-over-heels in love with me. Just because you're going through your pretty, charming, outwardly giving routine, I told myself sharply, doesn't mean a damn. He's probably not fooled by your act. People have a way of sensing when someone truly cares for them. Your expectations of him are out of line. And, I added, once again you're not looking at an individual as he really is. Here is Andrew, a remote, self-indulgent, moody, not overly affectionate person, and you're asking him to be totally different. *Impossible.*

But I was finding it difficult to be reasonable. It was a hot, muggy summer; friends were off to exotic resorts or European countries while I was stuck in the city. My son's absence deprived me of the distraction of his problems. I could fill my days with work, but there were the empty evenings and weekends that I felt unequal to handling. I wanted Andrew to banish loneliness from my life. I didn't want to have to look to my own resources. Did I have any resources? If I did I couldn't find them, or didn't know how to find them.

One evening as I sat in my rocking chair consumed with self-pity, wishing the phone would ring, I was suddenly flooded with memories of other days and nights of waiting. When I was very young, I waited for my mother or father to determine what my activities would be. There had been many of them: horseback riding, tennis, young people's concerts, young people's lectures, piano lessons, dancing lessons, acting lessons. My parents kept me busy; being inactive was wrong, sinful. Keep moving. Don't take time to think about what you really want. Don't take a chance of confronting anxiety or loneliness.

Later, with no practice in shaping my life, I waited for friends to call. I remembered my irritability and restlessness as I sat in my room, studying or reading or listening to the radio. I wanted something to happen, something marvelous and exciting that would relieve me of my uncomfortable emotions. And then—the ring of the phone. What a wonderful sound. Phone calls brought solutions. Wanna visit the La Brea tar pits tomorrow? We're all going to usher for the

Frank Sinatra concert, and we want you to do it, too. There's a party Saturday night. There's a beach party Saturday afternoon. Ice skating Friday night. Of course! I wanted to do them all! Those calls made me feel alive, popular, useful.

As a married lady I didn't have to wait for the phone to ring (a friend once observed that the best thing about marriage is that you always have a Saturday night date). But I waited for other things: for my husband to become perfect; for the two of us to share *everything*; for my husband to come home from work each night and give my life meaning; for other couples to invite us to fabulous parties; for something or someone to take away the emptiness that always seemed to haunt me.

And now here I was in my rocking chair—still waiting, waiting for magic.

But there is no magic, I told myself. There's only reality.

I hate reality. Reality means working and struggling and being alone. It's drudgery and pain.

And moments of joy.

Joy? Where is the joy?

Maybe if you stop looking for magic, you'll find it.

I tried to stop waiting that summer. With great effort I wrenched my attention away from the telephone and turned it inward. What did I want to do? I didn't know. Think! I urged myself. What is it you want? I demanded quick answers from myself, formulas for stamping out loneliness forever. When solutions weren't immediately forthcoming, I'd find myself wafting off into flights of fantasy where troubles and conflicts were unheard of. But those fantasies only left me clutching at froth—what could I do with that? I needed substance if I was to build my life, not bits of gossamer.

Hoping once and for all to confront loneliness and thus banish it forever, I spent a solitary weekend. During the two days I worked, walked in the park, and attended the ballet. I had been alone in the past, but always with my son around to break the silence, or with phone calls to and from friends to alleviate anxiety, to serve as anchors. That weekend I looked to no one. I was terrified that someone seeing me alone would think of me as unpopular, an outcast—would I ever be free of the worry of outside opinion? In addition, the act of being so completely solitary gave me all sorts of physical reactions: jumpiness, prickly, sensitive skin, pressure against my temples. But I was determined to see it through.

I found I was comfortable when I was completely involved in my thoughts or an activity. I had a lovely time at the ballet; I even derived pleasure from standing by myself and "people-watching" during intermission. But when I saw a couple I vaguely knew among the crowd, I became sick with envy. I darted furtively back to my seat lest they view me in my sorry alone state. After that the dancing appeared drab and colorless, and my walk home through steaming summer streets, surrounded by lightly clad amorous couples, was dismal.

During the afternoon on Sunday, I listened to the Fauré *Requiem* on the radio. I was transfixed. It was so beautiful. I was totally absorbed until a tiny part of my brain started me thinking how much better the moment would be if I had a special someone—Andrew—to share it with. In an instant I was shrouded in depression. Where was Andrew this weekend? Was he having a marvelous and glamorous time without me? As my thoughts went wild, the music that had so riveted my attention a minute ago played on to deaf ears.

So my experiment had failed. My confrontation with loneliness hadn't helped me to abolish it. But hadn't my therapist told me over and over that loneliness is a fact of life? ". . . part of the human condition. Once you can accept that," she had added, "then you can begin to find ways to cope with it. But don't deceive yourself that you can banish it, or that the way to cope is to attach yourself to another person. That never really works. Look to yourself for many ways of coping. Don't put all your hopes on one."

Okay, I acknowledged. Maybe one weekend isn't enough. Maybe it will take more looking inward. All right! I would continue to seek answers in myself. But I would also keep one eye focused out yonder—just in case.

Monday morning the phone rang. Oh, joy! It was Andrew. He hadn't forgotten me. Loneliness was temporarily something other people felt. I suggested we go to a Mozart and Haydn concert that week. Andrew thought it was a fine idea; he loved Mozart. It was decided I would pick up the tickets and we would meet near the box office on the appointed evening. After my solitary weekend, I eagerly looked forward to a shared experience.

The night of the concert Andrew was late—trouble at work, he informed me glumly as we hurried to our seats seconds before the first composition began. A knot of anxiety began to form in my stomach; already we were on different wavelengths. Andrew remained out of sorts throughout the early part of the evening, and I found myself concentrating on his mood, rather than on the music. Was he annoyed that he had to leave the unresolved problems at work just to meet *me*? Would he be able to enjoy the music that *I* had chosen? Would he find the performance accomplished enough for his sophisticated taste?

By intermission, Andrew appeared more relaxed. The Haydn was well done, he remarked, but he had reservations about the performance of the Mozart. He had heard it played far better many times before. Another pang! I had enjoyed the Mozart more than the Haydn. Nevertheless, I expressed agreement with Andrew. I was going to share at all costs.

After the concert I suggested we walk home, but Andrew, who still considered my neighborhood a den of thieves and muggers, all waiting beady-eyed and breathless in darkened doorways to pounce on his thousand-dollar wristwatch, insisted on taking a cab.

Oh, damn, I wailed inwardly, why can't he wear regular clothes like everyone else? Why the hell can't he be free enough to walk with me? He knows I love to walk. As I climbed into the taxi next to Andrew, I felt as abandoned and lonely as I had felt during my two days of solitude.

As the summer wore on, I was distressed to notice that Andrew was becoming increasingly remote and preoccupied. I couldn't figure out why. Outwardly we seemed to be getting along quite well—I hadn't articulated any of my disappointments to him, so why should he lose interest? I was dimly aware that he had some financial worries, concerns about his own self-esteem; he always talked big, but I could perceive that the talk covered up a lot of insecurity —anxieties about loneliness and fears of God-knew-what, but I couldn't comprehend why any of those should interfere with our relationship. If I was pretty, bubbly, and bright, available to mold and fit myself to what I imagined his needs to be, he should respond in kind.

Obviously Andrew didn't see it that way, for around the middle of September he stopped calling. I phoned him a couple of weeks later and, in my life-is-a-bowl-of-cherries soprano, inquired how he was. He replied that he was fine and wondered how I was, how my work was going. I sang out that everything was terrific. We agreed we'd have to get together soon. After I had chirped good-bye and hung up, I felt dreadful. It was all over. Why? What had I done? Was there something important I hadn't said? I was frantic to figure out what my mistake had been.

What's the big upset? my rational self wanted to know. You never liked him much anyhow.

We did have fun together.

Sure, you had fun, but you're acting as though you've lost your life raft. It's the end of a not very important relationship. It's not the end of the world. Who knows why he's no longer interested in seeing you? He may not know himself. It's not so different from what you went through with Stuart. He drifted off for his own reasons, and Andrew seems to have done the same. If you had looked at him a little more closely in the beginning, you'd probably have foreseen this.

Intellectually I had to admit that all of that made sense, but I couldn't help feeling lost and rejected. No more dreams of a perfect relationship. Back to work and child and my trembling alone self. It was too wearying to contemplate. It made me heavy and sad.

But the life force has a way of pulling one out of despair. My son was back, friends had returned, new articles were coming my way. There was less and less time for feelings of self-pity and remorse. Within two months Andrew had become a pale memory, a person who had occupied a very small space in my life for a very short time. Occasionally someone would mention his name, and then I'd wonder vaguely how he was getting on. What had I seen in him? I'd ask myself. It was so difficult to remember.

P.S. Andrew briefly popped back into my life two years later; he phoned me in October 1976. Our conversation went something like the following:

Scene takes place in Greta's study. Greta is at her typewriter.

Telephone on her desk rings.

> GRETA: (*Into phone*) Hello.
>
> ANDREW: (*His voice*) Hello, Greta.
>
> GRETA: Yes?
>
> ANDREW: This is Andrew.
>
> GRETA: Andrew who?
>
> ANDREW: Andrew N——.
>
> GRETA: You've got to be kidding.

ANDREW: I wonder if you'd like to have dinner with me.

GRETA: Are you crazy?

ANDREW: (*Puzzled*) Why do you say that?

GRETA: Two years ago you disappeared without even a good-bye, and now you're asking me to dinner without a word of explanation.

ANDREW: (*Surprised*) Oh, well, I was going through some difficult times then.

GRETA: Why didn't you tell me?

ANDREW: (*Vaguely*) Well, you know, there was another woman I was seeing as well as you.

GRETA: Yes, I remember. You told me she was pursuing you, and you couldn't stand her. I thought you had stopped seeing her.

ANDREW: Now, wait a minute. I didn't say I couldn't stand her. I just said I didn't much care for her.

GRETA: If you didn't much care for her, why did you continue to see her?

ANDREW: She was very persistent. I tried to break off with her, but she kept after me. It was hard to say no.

GRETA: Hmmmmm!

ANDREW: Besides, do you remember our last call?

GRETA: Not really.

ANDREW: Don't you remember? I said I wasn't feeling well, and you didn't even respond.

GRETA: I don't remember your telling me you weren't feeling well. If you had, I'm sure

I would have been in New Jersey in five minutes with chicken soup. Two years ago I was very big when it came to taking care of people.

ANDREW: Well, I didn't exactly say I wasn't feeling well. I said I was tired. You should have picked up on it.

GRETA: Why?

ANDREW: If you had been sensitive, you would have. The other woman did.

GRETA: Except you didn't like her. (*Silence*) If you had wanted me to know you weren't feeling well, you should have told me.

ANDREW: I expected you to get the message without my having to spell it out to you. Actually, I don't know exactly what happened with us. I always enjoyed being with you. We had fun. That's why I'd like to take you to dinner.

GRETA: I don't think I want to start anything again.

ANDREW: (*Hastily*) I'm not talking about an affair. I'm talking about dinner.

GRETA: I don't think so.

ANDREW: Would you mind telling me why?

GRETA: I guess I've changed. I'm looking for more directness in myself and others these days. You still seem to prefer the indirect approach.

ANDREW: I'm sorry you feel that way. (*Pleasantly*) Well, if you ever want to have dinner, give me a call. It would be nice to see you again.

GRETA: Good-bye, Andrew.

ANDREW: Good-bye.

GRETA: (*Hangs up phone and laughs. She speaks aloud.*) Now I know why he stopped calling. (*She looks puzzled*) Sort of. (*She laughs again, shrugs, and goes back to work.*)

Workshop III

Julia is not present tonight, so we proceed with just the six of us.

Connie starts off with good news. After last week's session she resolved to alleviate her work situation. Her first step was to ask to be transferred to a different department. To her astonishment, her request was immediately granted.

"It was easy," Connie relates, her voice bubbly and incredulous. "There was a lot of sympathy for my problem. I hadn't realized that my boss has a reputation for being difficult and competitive. It turns out she's a relative of someone important, so there's no way she can be fired. Apparently she's made a lot of people miserable, and everyone wondered how long it would take before I quit or asked for a change. Anyhow," she continues jubilantly, "I'm in a new department and it's great. I can't believe what it's done for me. For the past few months I could barely drag myself into work. Now I leap out of bed each morning, eager to get started." She smiles broadly. "I'm glad we talked last week."

I look at Connie and marvel; only twenty-four and she's managing her life in a very sensible way. Tonight, dressed in jeans, her long, dark hair pinned on both sides with barrettes, she looks like a teen-ager, but it's obvious she understands adult responsibilities better than many women in their thirties and forties.

Thirty-eight-year-old Laura's voice cuts through my thoughts: "It's terrific you had the guts to do that," she says enviously. "I wish I liked going to work. I hate my job."

Connie observes that Laura, too, could change jobs. She

says it was much easier to make a change than she had expected. "Thinking about it is worse than the actual doing. And," she adds, "the really good thing is that the new department offers many more advantages than the old one. That bitch did me a favor." She laughs. "Maybe I should thank her."

Laura replies that she can't change jobs so easily. "I get fantastic medical benefits. I don't know any other place that would pay part of my 'shrink' bill."

"You'll never know till you try," Ann remarks.

"And," I say, "even if you don't get the same benefits, if you have a more interesting job with a higher salary, you might consider it a fair trade-off."

"I don't know if I could do anything more than be a secretary."

Susan remarks that where she works there are training opportunities for those who want to go beyond being a secretary. She suggests Laura might find something similar. She also wonders if Laura's present place has opportunities for moving up. I am pleased to note that Susan seems less inclined to play the pretty young thing tonight.

Laura replies that there is no opportunity for advancement where she works. "It's a dead end," she adds sullenly.

"So why not look around?" is Connie's suggestion.

"Yeah. Maybe one of these days." Laura's expression becomes vague, and I figure she is about to put an end to the conversation in her usual abrupt fashion. She surprises me by continuing: "My mother would give me hell if I even mentioned changing jobs," she says. She nervously begins to twist one of her frizzy curls. "She doesn't want me to have a career. She wants me to get married."

I carefully remark that she mentioned her mother during our first session, and it was pretty clear then, as it is tonight, that she lets her mother decide what she should do with her life, rather than taking the responsibility for her own decisions.

"I don't *let* her," Laura retorts. "She calls me all the time. She doesn't leave me alone. If I tell her I'm going to buy new dishes, she tells me it's silly to buy dishes now, that I should wait until I get married. There's nothing I can do to stop her."

Connie wonders why she even tells her mother she's buying dishes.

Laura looks baffled and answers that she doesn't know why, that her mother had this way of getting her to reveal things.

I say: "Remember, Laura, during our first session we talked about the fact that we unconsciously control what we do. We say we want one thing, but our real goal is something else. We think we're victims, but actually we're calling the shots. That applies to you as well as to the rest of us. You say you don't want to talk to your mother. You say you don't like your job and you're only in it because of the benefits or because your mother thinks you should stay in it. But the truth is, for whatever the reasons, you're in the job because you've chosen it, and you talk to your mother because you choose to do so."

Laura makes a face. "I hate my job. I hate my mother."

I point out that, nevertheless, she has chosen to continue with the job and to keep up the interaction with her mother. She's not a victim, as she'd like to believe. "The most important thing you could get from these sessions," I continue, "is the understanding that you're making the choices. When you can finally acknowledge that you're in charge, you'll be in a much better position to decide if you want to go on in the old way or do something else that could be more rewarding."

"That's what my shrink says," Laura responds. "But how am I in charge when it's my mother who calls me, when it's my mother who won't leave me alone for a minute?"

"But you can choose whether or not you want to speak to her and what you want to speak to her about—if anything. Connie's right; you don't have to tell her you're buying dishes. As a child, you had to listen to her instructions, accept her intrusions, because you were dependent on her. But you don't need your mother in order to survive now. You can decide what's best for you."

"Yeah, yeah," Laura answers wearily. "You sound just like my shrink. Maybe I'll get it together one of these days. But the thought of talking back to my mother makes me so tired. I just want to fall asleep." And, indeed, she does seem to be drooping from exhaustion.

I quickly add that before she falls asleep I'd like her to understand that I'm not advocating that she talk back to her mother—this is not an assertiveness workshop. I just want her to begin to *think* about the fact that, even though she's a capable adult, she's still acting like mother's little girl. Out of habit, she's going through a routine she chose long ago to keep her mother from abandoning her. But since she no longer needs her mother to take care of her, she has the power to think about choosing new behavior.

Laura nods sleepily. I wonder if she even heard me.

Elaine, as bejeweled and elegantly dressed as in the first two sessions, points to Laura and confides that the way Laura looks now is the way she has been feeling most of the time lately. "My life is so empty," she declares sadly. "There's nothing to look forward to anymore. Before my daughter moved to New Mexico, we'd talk on the phone almost every day. We'd have lunch together a couple of times a week. We'd go to movies together. Now some mornings I think, why bother to get up? What's there to get up for? No child. No husband."

I am about to emphasize, as I have in other sessions, that Elaine's depression will only begin to abate when she stops dwelling on how others have deserted her and begins to make a life for herself.

Ann's voice stops me: "I felt like that when I broke up with my husband," she says softly. "There were days when I didn't get out of bed, and there were other days when I'd go through work like a zombie; then I'd come home and fall into a chair and stare at the walls. I wanted to keep myself anesthetized. I didn't want to have to face the pain. The only good thing about that period was that I didn't feel like eating, so I lost a lot of weight. As you can see, I had no trouble putting it back on." She smiles and pats her rounded hips.

Elaine wonders how she finally pulled herself together.

Ann replies that she's not sure. She thinks that one day she simply got sick of living like a robot. "I realized I was walking around like a dead person," she recalls, "and I figured I was wasting my precious life. I got mad at myself for going to pieces over someone who had been so mean to me. He was probably off having a great time, and I was practically committing suicide over him. I felt like a jerk. So I just started trying to revive myself. Whenever I'd begin to feel sorry for myself, I'd pull my attention to more constructive things: What did I want to do for me? How could I make my life better? It helped having a job to go to each day because it forced me to do something active. The weekends were the worst. And that's where my friends came in. They spent a lot of time with me. They tried to get me to do things. One of my friends was very helpful in talking to me about my marriage. She made me see that I really hadn't lost something wonderful, that I had always complained about my husband. She said she thought *I* had wanted to leave but hadn't had the guts, so I pushed my husband into doing it. She may be right. That whole period was sort of like learning to walk after being totally disabled. It was very painful and very tiring, and I needed a lot of assistance. But after about six months, I was strong enough to maneuver on my own."

I say that Ann has illustrated an excellent way of working through depression. She's shown us that there's no magic formula for "snapping out of it." There's a lot of thought and work involved. In fact, if we think we should feel better quickly, we become even more depressed when it doesn't happen.

Susan poses the question of why we get depressed in the first place, and Ann replies that she became depressed after her husband left her because she felt powerless. It seemed to her that when he walked out he took her identity with him.

I pick up on that and explain that a lot of depression comes from assuming all power emanates from someone else. We have nothing of our own. That sense of helplessness is what knocks us off our feet. I recall for them an interview I had with an actress who told me of being in a producer's office and talking to him about her career. Although no promises had been made, the actress believed the producer was interested in giving her a part in his next show. She felt this man was the key to her one big chance. They were getting along famously, and the actress was feeling good about herself, when the phone rang; it was another actor. The producer became involved in a long discussion with the other performer about his role in the show. Suddenly the actress felt wiped out. In her mind, the person on the phone was a star, while she was a zero. She sat numbly through the twenty-minute conversation, all the while wishing she could lie down on the carpet and die. After he hung up the phone, the producer was full of praise for the other actor. He went on at great length, and they somehow never got back to the actress and her career.

When she left the producer's office, the woman could barely maneuver her way home, and once there it took every ounce of her strength to get herself into bed.

I tell the women that when I mentioned to the actress that she needn't have sat there helplessly, she seemed puzzled. What could she have done? she wondered. I look around the room. "Do any of you see other options for her?"

"Sure," Connie responds. "She could have picked up and left when he didn't get off the phone in five minutes."

"She didn't have to be rude about it," Ann argues.

"Why not?" Connie comes back. "*He* was rude."

"Well, she didn't have to be rude, too. She could have

interrupted him nicely and asked if he was going to be long; if so, she'd make another appointment. Or she could have talked to his secretary and let her handle it."

"But if she had left," Elaine counters, "she might have ruined her chances for getting a part in the show."

"I don't think her chances were that good to begin with," is Connie's assessment.

Susan comments that no wonder she was depressed.

I remark that the actress became depressed because her lack of esteem for her own abilities made her look at the producer as some kind of saviour: her life depended on him—the old survival bit again—and therefore she must endure anything he dished out. If she had been clearer about her own capabilities, which are considerable, and her short and long-range goals, she would have taken the interview in stride—it was one of many. She would have felt free enough to ask herself if it was worthwhile waiting for him to get off the phone. How serious did she think he was about giving her the part in the show? She could have used the time while he was on the phone to think about some other alternatives—that way she wouldn't have gotten so involved in his conversation. When he began to praise the other actor, she could have told him gently but firmly that she was there to discuss her work, and could they please get back to that.

"Once you value yourself and your goals, it's much less likely that anything anyone else does or says will have the power to devastate you completely."

Laura, who seems to have perked up a bit, argues that you can't sit calmly and sort things out when you're feeling "shitty about yourself."

I agree with her and say: "Look, I know it's not easy to build self-esteem. In fact, it's excruciatingly hard. It's been a very long haul for me. If you've been put down most of your life, made to feel inadequate, you're not suddenly going to feel terrific, full of self-confidence. But you've got to start somewhere, and one of the best ways to raise self-esteem is to test yourself in a number of areas in order to see that the rest of the world doesn't view you as inept and inadequate. When you're out there trying new things, you'll discover what strengths you have. You'll become aware that the power is in you, not outside you. You'll see that you can have an effect. For example, Connie was feeling helpless about her job. She could have dragged along forever, filled with rage, depression, all sorts of non-productive emotions. Instead, she talked to us about it, thought about it, and then, even though she was a bit scared and hopeless, took some action. The result was that she discovered she could be very effective. Her boss wasn't such a powerhouse, after all. In addition, nothing awful happened; in fact, very positive things came out of her action. Now Connie has one bit of evidence that she's not helpless. And the next time something like this occurs, she'll be able to refer to the experience as a means of bolstering her self-confidence."

There is some general discussion about the business of sounding out ideas with friends, and Ann once again touts the advantages of her network of women friends. It's then that Susan breaks in to ask if we can go back to our discussion of self-esteem. The women agree, and Susan goes on to tell us that she considers it vital that men consider her pretty. She constantly wants to know that they're attracted to her.

"It's the only way I can feel good about myself," she confesses. "When I meet a man, and he doesn't flirt with me or let me know he thinks I'm really good-looking, I get depressed. I guess that's because I don't have a very high opinion of myself."

"From what you've said in the past two sessions," I reply, "I've gotten the impression you were brought up to be this cute, helpless creature whose only ability is to flutter her eyelashes and to get others to do things for her. That can't give you much self-confidence."

"It must be scary for you," comments Connie. "I would think you'd worry a lot about growing old and getting less pretty."

Susan acknowledges that she does worry but doesn't know how she can stop thinking about looks since she's been doing it for so many years.

I tell her that she can use the techniques we talked about in our first session to understand why she feels she has to be this pretty little thing, and then to see how it works against her as an adult. In addition, she can start to develop other strengths so she won't feel that her looks are all she has to offer. I reveal that I, too, was brought up to be pretty and popular, and there came a time when I decided that I didn't like the idea of my epitaph reading, "She was pretty and popular." I wanted my life to add up to more than that. That's when I began to change.

"When I think of the people I like most," interjects Ann, "I don't think of the best-looking ones. Looks pale after awhile. The best people are the ones you can talk to, who are intelligent, who will be there for you."

"I couldn't agree more," Connie states emphatically. "I know this really gorgeous woman; when you first see her you just can't take your eyes off of her. Then, after awhile, you get so bored. She doesn't even look beautiful anymore. No life comes out of her. She thinks she can be this perfect doll and that will be enough, and for some people it is enough. But who wants those people anyway?"

Elaine interrupts to remark that she doesn't think it's so terrible to be concerned about how you look. It's a fact of life that we're attracted to people who are handsome and pretty. She confides that she has been seriously considering having a face-lift. "Why not?" she asks defensively, before anyone can comment. "If my husband's not interested in me, maybe I'll meet someone else. Why not look as good as I can?"

"Except," argues Connie, "when you have a face-lift, you're implying that all you have to offer is your looks. And face-lifts don't last forever, so then you have to have another one, and then another one. And what about your body? How do you get your body to look as young as your face? It all sounds like a big bore."

"That's easy for you to say," Elaine replies irritably. "You're still in your twenties. You don't have to worry about looking older. You'll feel differently when you're in your fifties."

"I hope I don't. I hope by the time I'm in my fifties I'll have enough going for me so I won't mind looking older. I know some fabulous women in their sixties who have never had face-lifts and never will. I'd like to be like them."

Elaine turns to me and wonders if I ever think about having plastic surgery, now that I'm in my fifties.

I tell her that I've thought about it, but I've ruled it out. I explain that since I've found many other things in myself that I consider valuable and interesting, I don't want to return to the belief in the importance of looks—especially young looks. I add that I also don't like the idea of trying to kid myself that I can turn back the clock. I'm always a little suspicious of women and men who say that they have face-lifts, not because they want to look younger, but because they want to look as good as they can at any age. I think they really want to look younger. That way they can pretend they have some control over their destiny; they can give themselves ten extra years. Also, they're pandering to the notion that one is only attractive if one is wrinkle-free and young-looking.

"It's not a notion, it's true," Elaine protests. "People do look a lot better without wrinkles."

"I'm not so sure I agree with you," I respond. "Also, there comes a time when the skin on your face can't be stretched anymore without making you look as though you've been embalmed. At that point most people resign themselves to bags and wrinkles as the lesser of two evils. So why not go with nature right from the beginning?"

All the women seem fascinated by the subject of plastic surgery. Does a face-lift hurt? Ann wonders. I say that I've been told that it doesn't; nerves are cut so there's a feeling of numbness, rather than pain, after surgery. The nerves do regenerate, I assure her. Susan shudders and confides that she'd be frightened of something going wrong during the procedure. The risk seems to be minimal with a good plastic surgeon, is my reply. But it is major surgery. Connie mentions a woman at work who had a face-lift and expected everyone to compliment her on how great she looked; when no one even noticed a difference she was crestfallen. I recall running into a fifty-year-old man I hadn't seen for two years; I was shocked by his appearance. He had had one of those face-lifts where the skin is pulled very tight. He had always been interesting-looking, and now all the character had been stretched out of his face. I found it depressing, but apparently he was delighted. So who was I to criticize?

Elaine comments that I sound scornful of people who have plastic surgery, and I maintain that I'm not scornful, that I respect the right of anyone to do as he or she pleases. It's just not for me.

"Well," Elaine declares, smoothing her already smooth coiffure, "I feel young, so why shouldn't I look young? Why shouldn't my face go with my feelings?"

"I'm with Elaine," Ann says. "When the time comes, I'm pretty sure I'll have a face-lift. I like the idea of looking as good as you can for as long as you can."

Her statement seems to contradict her earlier comment that looks are unimportant, but I let it go. Instead, I emphasize that I just hate equating looking good with looking young. Then I warn them that not even the best face-lift will change their lives. "I've interviewed several plastic surgeons," I explain, "who have told me that the women who have expected their lives to be transformed as a result of having a younger-looking face have become terribly despondent when their lives have remained the same." I look at Elaine. "So if you do opt for plastic surgery in the near future, at least keep your expectations realistic. And," I conclude, "no matter what you do to your face, you're still going to have to set some goals for yourself, discover your skills, and take some risks. That's really where it's at in the long run."

Elaine nods vaguely but doesn't reply.

Our last discussion of the evening revolves around Susan. Looking embarrassed, she tells us that she feels silly making a big announcement, but she wants everyone to know that she finally filled out the school application and sent it off. She adds that she did it all by herself and then giggles.

We all laugh and applaud vigorously. Everyone compliments her, and it's clear that the praise is genuine. We are aware that doing that very simple task was a major effort for Susan.

"You must feel good," I say.

"I do." Susan beams happily.

"Once you got to it, was it very hard for you?" Ann asks.

"No. It was my imagination that made it into a terrible chore. Once I started, it was nothing. And here's a funny thing: my boyfriend was kind of surprised and annoyed because I didn't want him to help me. I was sort of thrown because I expected him to be pleased that I was doing something by myself."

I say that the incident shows why it has been so hard for her to move out on her own. The key people in her life haven't wanted her to. She has always picked people who have a need to direct all her activities.

Susan looks thoughtful. "I guess so."

"Did he get over being annoyed?" Ann inquires.

"Yeah, he did. I have to admit I got a little scared by his reaction. I don't want to lose him."

Connie comments that if she can lose him over something as small as filling out a school application, she'd be well rid of him. But the expression on Susan's face reveals that she's doubtful on that score.

I say that I concur with Connie, but I also understand Susan's fears. She believes she needs her boyfriend, as she needed her parents. Susan gives an affirmative nod of her head. But, I add, perhaps as she continues to demonstrate to herself that she can stand on her own two feet, she'll be less frightened of the possible consequences.

Ann suggests that, instead of leaving Susan, her boyfriend could very well decide to change himself. "I like to look on the positive side," she remarks with a smile.

It is then agreed that Ann's positive thinking should be the last word of the evening. Everyone wants an upbeat ending.

I review the session on the way home. Ann was much more involved with the others tonight—even revealed things about herself. She was insightful about her feelings of depression, and I imagine she gave the group some interesting things to think about. I hope so. How nice that Connie was able to effect a change at work. I am also pleased that Susan questioned her dependence on her looks. I know from experience that that's a hard one to overcome. And isn't it great that she was able to push herself to do the school application? I do wonder, however, about Elaine and Laura. They are both stuck with the very deep belief that they are victims. According to them, everything that happens in their lives is someone else's fault. Neither seems willing to go beyond that assumption.

I think back to the days when I felt like a victim and acknowledge how difficult it is to realize that there are always *some* alternatives, even when things seem terribly hopeless. I remember twenty-eight-year-old Sandy from a previous workshop. She was in the depths during the first session. Her husband had left her for another woman, and there she was with two small children, almost no money, and very few marketable skills. "I cry every day," she had told us. She was sure there was no hope for her. She was convinced she couldn't possibly manage alone—"I've never been alone in my life," she had sobbed. The only solution she could come up with was to get her husband to come back to her. Another woman in the workshop, who had gone through a similar experience, had spoken to her from across the room in the softest, kindest voice. "Yes, it's awful," she had almost whispered, "but I promise you it will get better. You're stronger than you think you are." Sandy had wept and shaken her head stubbornly.

But by the third session, she was no longer weeping. She couldn't afford to. Out of necessity, she had begun to take her life in hand. She was finding there were options—not perfect ones, but there were things she could do. She had found a job—"It sure isn't my dream job," she had commented grimly, "but at least I have some money coming in." She had also found an older woman in the neighborhood who, for a very small sum, would care for the children during the day while she was at work. It was hard, and it was lonely, but she was no longer the beaten, devastated woman of the first session. By our fifth session, Sandy went so far as to suggest that maybe everything had happened for the best. She had always been a compliant wife, and now she was finding it awfully nice to be the boss. Yes! She was feeling a little bit hopeful. She had dazzled us with the brightest of smiles.

I sigh pleasurably. It's a nice memory. I'd love to be able to persuade Laura and Elaine to look more to themselves for ways of handling their problems. I even mentioned my concern for them to my therapist. She reminded me that all I could do was present them with ideas and suggestions;

the rest was up to them. "You can't force anyone to change," she had said. True! Ah, well! We still have two more sessions.

As I walk along, I think about Sandy and wonder how she's getting on.

Chapter V

A very happy thing has just occurred; my husband
has given the go-ahead sign on fixing up the bedroom. I can start off with two hundred dollars, and
he has promised to sign this so that he won't go
back on his word. The next thing you see will be his
official signature.
—From my Journal, October 15, 1957

Through all the "Sturm und Drang" of relationships and
confrontations with my son, I continued to work. I had
to. For the first time in my life I had large financial responsibilities. I needed money.

In one sense, that necessity had a positive effect: it forced
me to discipline myself; it made me move; it encouraged
me to take risks I would normally have avoided. But it also
brought inordinate anxiety. I felt myself being buried alive
beneath an avalanche of monthly bills. So intense was the
emotion that sometimes the act of writing a check left me
gasping for breath.

It wasn't that I didn't have the ability to earn a living. I
did. But I had no backlog of experience to bolster my confidence in that ability. I had never supported myself beyond
a bare survival level. Therefore, each day I'd go through
the motions of being a wage earner, and each day, with
racing heart, I'd ask myself the same questions: Can I do
it? Can I take care of myself and a child? How long before
the weight of responsibility crushes me completely?

And yet, work was not new to me. I had always worked.
During my high school years in Los Angeles, I clerked or
wrapped packages at various department stores on Thursday

nights and Saturdays. After college, before leaving for New York, I was a drama teacher in an after-school program. But I can't recall what I used my earnings for. I don't remember managing money, saving it for something special or learning the value of it.

My money was play money. Real money, important money, came from my parents. Part of their power was their control of finances. My father kept his earnings a secret; there was no need for the children to know about money problems; he would provide for us. But I could see that money made my mother and father anxious—especially my mother. They didn't part with it lightly. They let my sister and me know that money was for necessities, not for frivolities. The trouble was, one couldn't always differentiate between the two.

"Can you afford a new dress for me?" I'd ask my mother.

A pained look would cross her face. "If you *really* need it, you can have it," she'd answer.

"But can you afford it?"

"If you really need it, we'll have to manage."

I'd watch her furrowed brow with a sense of doom. They couldn't afford it. I was being self-indulgent. I didn't *really* need it. That dress my cousin had outgrown would fit me adequately. Then I'd groan inwardly. I hated that dress. But dared I put a financial burden on my parents? My mother had said they could manage, but I wasn't too sure she had meant it. It was frightening to imagine that my getting a dress might plunge us all into poverty.

When I suggested to my parents that I work full-time during the summer in order to pay for my own clothes, they were aghast. They could take care of me. I didn't have to work long hours at such a demeaning job. I should do things that gave me status, that had some element of glamour about them. Work full-time in a department store? I can still see the curl of my mother's lip. Besides, she had lined up a drama class for me, so much more interesting than working in a department store.

I decided I would be an actress. My mother loved the theater and movies. She adored Katharine Cornell and Katherine Hepburn, and she thought Hedy Lamarr was gorgeous. I had the impression she wanted me to be a combination of all three. Ah, but I shouldn't have to work too hard at it. I should do everything easily. None of my endeavors should take too much time away from the anxious demands of my parents at home.

And I honestly believed it would all be effortless. I wore my shoulder-length black hair parted in the middle, arched my eyebrows, widened my mouth with crimson lipstick, took drama lessons, and waited to be discovered. Nothing happened (unless you count being tapped for the temple choir by the rabbi of the Olympic Jewish Center as being discovered).

"If I had your looks," my mother repeated over and over, "I'd be a star."

It was all *my* fault, then, that I hadn't been discovered. *She* would have been discovered. *I* was doing something wrong. I wasn't living up to my potential. I was a failure. I wasn't making magic happen.

Maybe I was in the wrong place. Maybe it would happen in New York. I didn't have to be a movie star; I could work in the legitimate theater, the way Katharine Cornell did.

In 1951, at the age of twenty-three, with nine hundred dollars stashed in my purse, I took off for the big city. Two weeks after my arrival, I "fell in love" with a successful television writer and moved in with him—so much easier than going apartment hunting in a strange and terrifying metropolis. When I mentioned to my lover that I would get a job, he curled his lip in a very familiar way. An office job? He thought I wanted to be an actress.

Well, I did need to make money.

Whatever for? He had enough for both of us.

That was true. He did. Okay! I'd work in a small Greenwich Village theater company instead. Again the curled lip. Didn't I want to be the best? To be on Broadway? What did that scruffy group have to do with the "real theater?"

I felt embarrassed even to have thought of it. I enrolled in an acting class and began to make the rounds of Broadway and television producers.

Six months later, when we split up, my nine hundred dollars was gone, and it was get work or starve.

For the next five years, I lived in a thirty-eight-dollar-a-month tenement apartment and went through an assortment of part-time and temporary jobs. I typed, waited tables, cashiered, modeled, worked conventions, and sold. But I always made it extremely clear that I did not belong in any of those positions; I was an "actress" trying to make ends meet—which is just about all I did—until the big break came. The tenement was only temporary, until my ship came in.

I began to get a few acting jobs—summer stock, television, off Broadway, and ultimately Broadway. But acting was never serious business for me. It was fantasyland, glamour, an escape from reality. And I never ever let it distract me from the current man in my life. Theater was status, but a man was survival.

After my marriage, I stopped the part-time work and concentrated on theater and television. But the conflicts! My home and husband were my anchors. I couldn't take any chance of losing them. It was seventeen years of feeling pulled, twisted, split in half. At times I wondered if I were going mad. When I didn't work as an actress, I was identity-less, a nothing, a cardboard figure who could easily be discarded on the junk heap. When I was in a show, and being "someone," I trembled lest I lose my moorings. Wasn't being unavailable tantamount to treason? Didn't I deserve to be abandoned? During a six-month run in a Broadway show, I rushed home between each matinee and evening performance in order to cook my husband supper. I think now I also wanted to make sure he was still there.

Four years before my marriage ended, I gave up the fight. It was too much. I was beaten and tired. I would devote my greatest energies to being a wife and mother. The theater would have to get on without me.

Under the tutelage of my editor-writer husband, I began to do a bit of writing. It was safer: I could stay home; make my own hours; be available. I dabbled: a few book reviews, some innocuous articles. I was playing at being a journalist.

And then, in January 1974, playtime was over. It was time to grow up.

I took any article assignments I could get. I called everyone I knew and asked for work. I felt shy and uncomfortable in presenting myself as a professional writer, but necessity made me bold. I thought about a full-time job. What could I do? I could type. A shudder of revulsion. Would I have to return to the scrounging woman I had been in my twenties? Would I end up in a different office each week, typing labels and legal briefs, working for a salary just above the minimum wage? Was that all I was good for after so many years? Better to pursue the writing.

I let my son know that money was tight, that we couldn't spend as we had in the past. Not that I had ever been extravagant; with my upbringing, that was out of the question. But I had been freer when I could depend on my husband's regular income. Now I was beset with all my mother's questions and fears. I wanted stereo equipment—my husband had taken ours—so I could listen to my records. Instead of looking at my checkbook and savings to see what I could afford, I went into the automatic routine: Did I *really* need it? Wouldn't I be out on the street carrying all my possessions in shopping bags if I indulged myself? And didn't I have a perfectly good radio? How frivolous of me to want stereo equipment as well. It was absolutely not a necessity and would have to wait.

My attitude was even more extreme whenever I'd take my son out to dinner. If I treated him to a meal at a Chinese restaurant—ten dollars for the two of us—I'd be unable to enjoy myself fully because I was so nervous he'd order more than I could afford, an extra bowl of rice, perhaps. I hated myself for my unreasonable penury, especially since it reminded me of my mother's behavior when she and my father would take my sister and me out to dinner. In those days the restaurants had charged extra for milk; therefore, my sister and I were admonished not to order it. "We have plenty of milk at home," my mother would declare. "No sense paying extra for something you can have when you get home."

Such craziness she had passed on to me! Those insane fears blinded me to reality.

In truth, most of the first year wasn't too bad financially. I managed to get enough assignments to keep me going, and I was able to finish my book.

To a large extent, the book was instrumental in opening my eyes to the importance and the realities of work. The ten women I had profiled all had thriving careers: one was the highest-ranking policewoman in the New York City police force, another a prominent attorney. I had included an opera orchestra conductor, a doctor, an editor and leading feminist, a television producer, among others.

Unlike me, these women had been encouraged by their parents to enter the labor force. They hadn't been fed a lot of nonsense about glamour and status. They had not believed their survival depended on attaching themselves to "Mr. Right." They had always assumed that whether they married or not, and several were married with children, they would have careers that excited them and supported them; one of the women had been virtually self-supporting since the age of thirteen. For all of them, work was a combination of necessity and pleasure. It provided an important focal point for their lives.

Moreover, the women had always understood that success in work comes slowly and with a great deal of trial and error. None of them had ever expected to be "discovered." The idea of quick answers and facile solutions was foreign to them.

I could see that I had a long way to go if I were to emulate them—and I did want to emulate them; they were as much role models for me as they were for my young-adult readers. I would have to teach myself the attitudes toward work that were ingrained in them. I would have to divest myself of my old automatic behaviors and beliefs. I knew I could never reach the successes they had built up over periods of fifteen to twenty years, but I could build something. It wouldn't be easy, but it wasn't impossible.

As the year progressed my assignments became more varied. During the summer I picked up work writing publicity pieces for a non-profit organization, and in September I did a script for a producer of audio cassettes. My script would teach doctors' nurses how to collect delinquent fees; it wasn't high drama, but I was in no position to be choosy. When I spoke to the producer, he inquired if I had ever written anything similar. No, I hadn't, but if he would teach me I could learn—I hoped he'd take me under his wing and become my mentor, as my husband had. He didn't see any need to teach me, he replied, smashing all my dreams of leaning on his strong shoulder; I could learn by writing it. He gave me a sample script, the material he wanted included in my script, and sent me on my way.

And I wrote it. Not easily, as I had assumed everything should be done, but through long hours of labor. More evidence that my mother had been wrong. People didn't just toss things off and get paid thousands of dollars for them. They worked like crazy and often got very little for their pains—three hundred dollars this go-round. It was a blooming struggle.

On the other hand, I had acquired a new skill. The producer recorded my script with one of the top commercial voice-over actresses doing all the parts. It wasn't Chekov, but it sounded terrific to me. One of the best cassettes we've ever produced, was the verdict. I glowed.

I was making it. It was going to be all right. That was in October. By the end of November, I was singing the I'm-falling-apart blues. Where was the money that was owed me? Why hadn't the checks arrived in the mail? Why were there no new assignments? The holidays were coming, and I was broke. What was going on? I was scared out of my skull.

In January, an article I had been working on for several months was killed (not accepted) by the magazine that assigned it. That meant that I would receive a "kill-fee"—25 percent of the total fee—instead of the full amount. My first rejection. I was ruined, finished. I had been counting heavily on the full payment; without it I'd never make it. And if the piece was unacceptable, didn't that mean my writing was inadequate? The final proof that I was a pretender. I went into a depression. I dragged around the house, unable to function with any effectiveness. My brain, which had been so fertile throughout the year, seemed suddenly to have dried up; hard as I tried, I couldn't wrench a single idea or creative thought from it.

"What's happening to me?" I cried to my therapist, my voice rising in panic. "I thought I was doing so well, and now I've become a failure."

"It's not that you're a failure," she answered. "It's simply that you haven't provided yourself with any alternatives. You're frightened because you think you have no other options. You're in a field where checks can be late, assignments irregular, where work is rejected for all sorts of reasons having nothing to do with your ability. You have to understand that and make other provisions for those times. You were lucky most of the year, but you can't count on luck being constant. You have to think about your work; you have to make plans."

She was right, as usual. I had taken on assignments mindlessly, assuming that everything would go along on an even keel. I had made no plans, had set up no contingencies. Instead of taking control, I had left everything to chance.

But where to start? Start with the immediate necessity, counseled my rational self. You need money. Yes, I did, desperately. My empty checking account prevented me from thinking of anything else. But where to get it? I had put out feelers for a full-time job, but there was nothing in the offing. Again I thought of working as a typist, and again I rejected it. To do that would represent complete defeat, I felt. I could borrow money; that was a possibility.

It was then I heard my mother's voice: Won't you sink yourself in debt? Don't go in over your head. What makes you think you'll ever make enough to pay back the loan?

You've got to believe in yourself, urged my rational self. If you don't, no one will. Start small. Just borrow enough so you can relax and plan.

I borrowed from my friends. They were delighted to help me out. "Take your time paying us back," they said.

With temporary relief from money worries, I began to think about my career. First of all, given the uncertainties of free-lancing, did I want to continue? There were certainly more reliable ways of earning a living. I decided that I did want to continue. The year had shown me that I functioned well in an unstructured setting. I didn't need someone to set hours for me; I was disciplined enough to structure my own workday. I especially loved the idea of being able to take off on a Tuesday and to make up the time on a Sunday. I was willing to accept the insecurity in exchange for my freedom —even though freedom often meant working fourteen hours a day, seven days a week.

I thought about ways of increasing my stability. Article writing was fine, but it had its limitations. One was always wracking one's brain for new ideas, then trying to sell the ideas to the appropriate publication. In addition, no money crossed your palm until the piece was accepted—*if* the piece were accepted.

A book offered more possibilities. For one, there was an advance payment against earned royalties. That offered some cushion during the months of work. Then there were royalties. A friend of mine who wrote children's books had told me that her books had been earning royalties for over ten years. And her income was impressive. I recognized that a great many books don't earn a penny beyond the advance, and that children's books don't ever make as much as a successful adult book, but it was an option worth exploring. If I could produce several young-adult and children's books, they might serve as a future annuity. And since I had just completed one young-adult book, it shouldn't be too difficult to come up with another.

Last of all, I determined to seek out more publicity writing, rather than rely on only one source. And I could look into writing foundation reports, as well as part-time and per diem jobs.

The more I thought about my various options, the less panicked I was. I was in charge. I wasn't waiting for someone out there to send checks or come up with assignments. I had things to do, ideas to pursue. I was taken out of the realm of vague anxiety into the area of thought and action. As a result, my dormant brain began to wake up, and my body, as though given a shot of adrenalin, began to move briskly instead of flopping around like Raggedy Ann. Within three months, I had gotten an advance to do a career-guide book for junior-high-school boys and girls, had landed a two-month job for April and May, and had lined up a couple of article assignments.

As soon as I stopped worrying about them, the checks that had been owed me arrived in the mail. I quickly repaid the loan—cross off one debt I wouldn't sink under. I was back in the running. I wasn't yet ready to be counted out.

Chapter VI

To be oneself is the hardest thing of all. A dozen times a day I peer anxiously into the mirror, dissatisfied because I look like me and not like someone else. Every day I demand the impossible: to be me and yet to be another person. And how inconstant I am, for I am not even faithful to one image but change with the fashion of the day. I pine to be utterly, devotedly, single-mindedly, me.

—From my journal, September 30, 1960

My second year as a woman alone was under way. Looking back, those first twelve months didn't seem too awful. True, they hadn't been composed of great triumphs, but there had been small successes. I had taken a more realistic approach to the business of earning a living, had set down a few rules as a parent, and had survived, and even profited from, a lonely summer and two disappointing relationhips.

But now that the immediate pressures had begun to abate, other problems were emerging from the shadows in increasingly defined forms. The most important of them was my sense of low self-esteem.

I had always been aware that I viewed other people as powerful and gifted, while I saw myself as second-rate. I was okay as long as my advice and help were needed. Then I had the illusion of being pretty terrific—superior, even: I could cope with emergencies; I was good at picking up everybody's pieces; I had solutions for everyone else's problems. But without my props, self-esteem went out the window. I had taken for granted that one day, with a string

111

of accomplishments in my bow, I would feel equal to the exalted others; at last I would be truly worthy of friendship and high regard.

Alas, that day of equality always seemed to be in the future. In my eyes, nothing I did was ever significant or valuable enough to elevate me to a higher plane. I inevitably fell just short of the mark. When my book came out in June of that second year, although I secretly hugged it lovingly to my breast, I was somewhat ashamed of presenting it to the world. It was for young people; important books were for adults. I had written in simple sentences, while other writers broke literary ground with dazzling prose.

I thought about giving friends copies of my first hard-cover publication, as they had given me copies of theirs, and then dismissed the idea. I doubted any of them would want a "young-adult" book. Then they'd feel compelled to read it and to comment on it. I didn't want to put anyone in the embarrassing position of having to lie to me. To my distress, a few friends went out and bought the book, while others checked it out of the library. One man, whose literary opinion I valued highly, wrote me a warm and complimentary letter. I was deeply touched, yet questioned his sincerity. Was he just trying to make me feel good? No, that wasn't his way; he was intensely honest, especially when it came to books. Maybe his note was sincere, but could it be that in this case he had been deceived? His words of praise made me uncomfortable.

I was far more comfortable with a putdown. Putdowns had been my bread and butter for as long as I could remember. True, they gave me pain, but they were so recognizable, so familiar. They didn't fill me with anxiety-provoking questions that came with praise.

"Look how graceful Jennie is," my mother had repeated ad nauseam during my early grammar-school years. "Doesn't she have a lovely singing voice? She's so talented at the

piano. Of course, you do very nicely, too, but Jennie has a
way about her."

My mother told me that my seventh-grade friend, Virginia, was such an excellent student, so well dressed, so
very friendly—"Why must you always be sarcastic?"

In high school, Margo had incredible taste in clothes—
"Must you wear your skirts so short?"—and such a lovely
figure—"Your thighs will be heavy like mine." Louise's hair
resembled spun silk—"It looks as if you have a rat's nest in
your pompadour." Sharon was so talented at the piano and
what a wonderful actress—"You were nice in the play, dear,
but wasn't Sharon breathtaking?" My father thought that
Jackie was fantastic looking, and my mother observed that
Barbara knew the perfect way to talk to boys—"You sound
stiff and awkward. No wonder you're not as popular as you
should be."

I tried to be like all of them, rebelled at having to be like
all of them, wept at not being able to become like any of
them.

My eyes were ever trained outward. Therefore, there was
no possible chance of developing a very special and unique
me. Everything about me, from clothes and hair to my ideas,
was copied; I was a frantic imitator. And still I never seemed
to measure up.

When I was in the theater, I went into a hit Broadway
show in a featured part for the last half of the run. It was
a reasonably funny play and a very nice role. I received a
lot of newspaper publicity, and during my six-month stint,
a larger-than-life picture of me graced the front of the
theater. In addition, everyone complimented me on my performance.

Question: What actress could ask for more?

Answer: This actress.

It really isn't a very good show, I told myself. It's not
Chekov. It's not Shakespeare. It's not even Arthur Miller

or Tennessee Williams. If I were a really good actress, I'd
have been cast in a play of more merit. Anybody could do
this part. If I get sick, my understudy will be smashing.
I'd better not get sick. I watched other members of the
cast: they were good; I could never hope to equal them.

The lack of confidence permeated every area of my life. If
I gave a dinner party, I worried about the food; all the other
women I knew were such fabulous cooks. I anguished over
the guest list; God forbid they might not all get on perfectly,
another example of my doing something inadequately.

When it came to expressing convictions, whether political,
literary, or psychological, I quoted others in a loud, argu-
mentative voice. I never discussed quietly: I couldn't; my
convictions didn't come from any inner thought process,
they were borrowed from people I assumed had all the
answers. I couldn't logically substantiate my claims, so I de-
fended them noisily. I can recall having a heated argument
with a man over the literary merits of Graham Greene. I expressed vigorous anti-Greene sentiments for a good twenty
minutes, at which point the man, an ardent Greene fan, wondered how many Graham Greene books I had read. One, I
confessed, and I had just skimmed it. The man walked away
from the argument in disgust. (Since then, I have read all of
Graham Greene's books and have thoroughly enjoyed most
of them. Obviously, during that long-ago argument I was
parroting my current "authority figure.")

Because I had no concept of who I was, what I could do,
and what I believed, I was in awe of everyone: couples
who seemed happily married; beautiful women; intelligent
women; talented women; feisty women; intelligent men; famous people; people who seemed very sure of themselves;
my son's teachers.

I wasn't intimidated by all of them all of the time, but it
took very little to activate my feelings of insecurity. When a
photographer friend related how an art director had en-
thused over her work, I crumbled; no one was throwing ac-

colades my way. A screenwriter boasted of her competitive streak, and I felt diminished: I hated competition because I expected to lose; this "giantess" knew she'd win. Should "famous" friends invite me out, or to their homes, I unquestioningly accepted. I considered myself lucky that they were interested in me at all. I also made sure I kept in touch with *all* my friends; if they didn't hear from me, they might forget all about me.

I wanted my son's teachers to think I was a nice person, a "good mother," so whatever they suggested I agreed to— even when my strong instincts argued against them. How could I defy the experts? (Some of those experts were all of twenty-five.)

Throughout most of 1975, I was "romantically" involved with a businessman named Josh. (I had entered the relationship in the usual heedless fashion.) Josh continually expressed firm opinions on a variety of subjects: how to be a "good parent"; how to be successful in business; what constitutes good manners; how to deal with problems in relationships. I had reservations about his pronouncements, but because they usually were aimed at demonstrating to me how I was doing everything wrong, I most often ended up wallowing in a little pool of self-doubt. Days later, I'd recognize that his sensible lectures were actually disguised put-downs, and I'd rage inwardly and impotently.

"You've got to stop taking people at face value," my therapist advised me. "Just because someone says he or she has all the answers, or is happy and strong and trouble-free, doesn't make it so. You must begin to really listen to people. You owe it to yourself and to them to observe them as three-dimensional individuals, rather than stick figures. And you have to start giving value to your own very sound judgment and your very real accomplishments."

One night in August, I sat in my rocking chair and tried to follow her advice. I thought about the photographer: her career was hardly meteoric; it was having the same ups and downs as mine. Her boasts were often attempts to present a successful facade when she was feeling a failure. Still, her work was good; why shouldn't people enthuse over it? On the other hand, compliments didn't always guarantee a sale; the art director, who had been so impressed with the photographer's work, hadn't come through with an assignment. But why should I feel eclipsed by my friend's achievements, anyhow? I had achievements of my own. Magazines were paying money for my articles, and money went a lot farther than compliments.

And come to think of it I had been getting my share of praise; how like me to forget. My book was receiving good reviews, and I had gotten some very nice responses from readers of all ages. An article I had written on jealousy—an emotion I knew only too well—had produced a flurry of letters; all had been complimentary, and all had said that the piece had made them less ashamed of their jealous feelings and had helped in coping with them. And only a week ago, at lunch, a magazine editor for whom I had great respect had suddenly said to me: "You do know you're good, don't you?"

I had been taken aback. "Good?" I had never dared think about it.

"But you are," she had persisted. "Your research is thorough, you write clearly and informatively, you meet your deadlines, and your copy needs very little editing. That's better than most."

I hadn't quite believed her. How could I be better than most when I grew up believing everyone else was better than I? "Not everyone has the need to put you down as your parents did," would be my therapist's reply to that one. Maybe so. The editor had always been completely honest when she hadn't liked something, so why shouldn't she be equally sincere in her praise? Despite my doubts, I had to admit it made sense.

Next, I looked at "famous" friends. With all their successes, they were as much a part of the human condition as I was; they worried, got sick, felt anxious and depressed, had problems with relationships. And why did I assume they were doing me a favor by calling me and, therefore, I must jump at their command? I was hardly a pitiable creature they had to rescue. Quite the opposite. Since separating from my husband, I had become increasingly self-sufficient, more sure of my own opinions and values. I no longer argued noisily and mindlessly, quoting everyone else's ideas. Thanks to my rocking-chair sessions, I had learned to think things through, to use my own judgment in order to come to conclusions. Why did I feel I was so forgettable? It was time to find out if my assumptions were true.

Last of all, I took a hard look at Josh. What had compelled me to stay in this relationship for eight months? I mean, let's face it, Josh walked in my parents' shoes: he was always putting me down and I was always angry at him; he had a million problems and anxieties; and although he had self-help formulas for every eventuality, he barely maneuvered his own life. Sure, he could talk glibly about how well he got on with his kids; he saw them once or twice a month for a couple of hours—during which time they usually played Scrabble. Who wouldn't get on with their kids under those circumstances? What else but masochism made me run to him with my mothering problems? The script was predictable; he would point out how I was failing as a parent and how fantastic he was. Did I need that? Besides, if he was so superb with children, why was it that he got on so abysmally with my son? I had asked him dozens of times not to put my son down, not to be a disciplinarian with him. That was my job. But Josh had never listened. Since he was the adult, he felt he had the right to order my son about. Needless to say, my son couldn't stand him.

To be honest, I had stuck with Josh because he had stuck with me. He hadn't been unavailable as Stuart and Andrew

had been. He called regularly—you could set your watch
by his calls—was on time for dates, and brought me very
nice presents. I had settled for the trappings because I still
believed I needed a man in my life for self-esteem. Ironically, my self-esteem plummeted when I was with Josh.
Not only because he was always criticizing me, but because
I couldn't respect myself for spending so much time with
a person I didn't like.

I made three resolutions that evening in August: to break
with Josh; to take time before entering another relationship; to get together with friends because I wanted to be
with them on that particular day or evening, not because
I was afraid they'd drop me or forget me.

It took me a month to summon up the courage to tell
Josh we were through. I was so fearful of hurting him. I
waited for the perfect moment. In September, when that
moment still hadn't materialized, I tearfully and imperfectly
blurted out the sad news over the phone. Josh was stunned,
speechless, he had no idea . . . ! He'd have to call me
back. I wept copiously after I hung up, certain I had de-
stroyed the poor man. What a shock it was to hear Josh's
cheery voice a few hours later. He had just landed a fantastic new account, he informed me. He felt great and didn't
have time to mourn the end of our relationship. Was I all
right? I sounded a little teary. He ended by telling me to
let him know when I'd like to come by his house and pick
up the few things I'd left there. "I look forward to seeing
you," were his parting words.

Schmuck, I berated myself. "And you were afraid of
hurting his feelings. Dry your tears and get on with your
life."

True to my resolve, I became more selective about my
socializing. I didn't have to run when people called. I discovered that, although it made me inordinately anxious,
I could say no if I felt like staying home without friendships dissolving in the air. Being on tap was obviously not

a requisite, as I had assumed. Could it be that I had more
to offer than availability? Maybe.

I must confess that the unaccustomed staying home made
me very nervous. What would people think? That I was
unpopular? And, indeed, I was staying home a great deal.
With Josh out of the picture, and without the compulsion
to keep on the go, I often found myself on a weekend night
curled up with a good book, listening to music on the radio
—still no stereo.

On one such Saturday night, my son sidled into the living
room and said casually: "My friends wonder why you don't
go out much. Why don't you? Other parents go to parties
on Saturday nights."

Terror! My worst nightmare come to pass! He and his
friends had been talking about me. They had seen the real
me: an outcast; a wallflower; unpopular! Other parents led
exciting lives, while I, a drab, unwanted creature, sat home
alone.

Wait! Wait! cried my rational self. Nobody has rejected
you. You chose to stay home. Remember? You're not a poor
thing. Your son is not your mother. You don't have to copy
others to impress him. That never worked, anyhow; no
matter how hard you tried, your mother still compared you
unfavorably with your girlfriends. Forget the old act. Have
the courage to be yourself.

And so I looked my son in the eye and said: "Just because
other parents go out on Saturday night doesn't mean I have
to. Lately I've felt like staying home. When I feel like going
out, I will."

"Who will you go out with?" was his next thrust. "Since
you and Josh split up, you don't have a boyfriend."

After I had pulled myself psychologically up off the floor,
I replied as coolly as I could: "I haven't met anyone I care
about. That's why I don't have a 'boyfriend.' But I don't
need a man in order to go out. I can manage very well
alone or with a woman friend."

He thought about that for a minute, then said: "I just don't see why anybody would *want* to stay home on a Saturday night."

Now with genuine cool: "Maybe one of these days you'll be tired of all the Saturday night parties, and you'll want to stay home occasionally."

"Maybe." He shrugged and abruptly left the room.

Once he was gone, I smiled weakly at my triumph. I had apparently convinced him of my strength and confidence in my decision. Now all I had to do was convince myself.

During my August rocking-chair session, I hadn't given much thought to the subject of my son's teachers. It had been summer vacation, and therefore no school problems had arisen. But once the new term began, I was offered ample opportunity to face the issue head-on. In November, I went in for the routine meet-the-new-teacher visit. I was greeted by a young woman who quickly informed me that she and my son got on extremely well—"I mother him," she told me smugly. She then launched into a long analysis of my son's "problems and insecurities." My gut instinct was to stop her and say that I wasn't there to discuss "problems and insecurities," that I was more aware of them than she was, and that I wanted to know how he was doing in math, English and history. I didn't want to antagonize her, however, so I waited for her to bring up the academics. Somehow, she never got to them. Her main goal appeared to be to let me know that she understood my son, and obviously I didn't.

And still I didn't protest. I felt too guilty, too inadequate. She was the "good mother," and I was the "bad mother." At the end of the interview, I thanked her politely for all her advice and went home in a rage.

The interview stayed with me all day. I hadn't liked myself for remaining mute. I really didn't approve of using the classroom as a place to air personal travails; it was inappropriate and harmful. In addition, it took away from teach-

ing time. That night I wrote the teacher a letter explaining
my point of view. I reasoned that such an approach was particularly wrong for my son, since he reveled in delineating
all his problems—he was not above making some up if he
ran short. What he needed, I added, was more emphasis
on doing well in his studies. He should be encouraged to
get his papers in on time, to come prepared for tests, to pay
attention in class, to observe the rules. I concluded by saying that I was aware of any problems he might have and
was working to correct them. Therefore, she could concentrate on teaching the various subjects.

After posting the letter, I began to tremble. How dared
I be so presumptuous as to tell a teacher what her job was?
I should never have opposed her. She'll turn my son against
me forever; she'll use her power to wipe me out of the picture.

My rational self argued that I had done the right thing,
that I had a responsibility to my son to speak up against
ineptitude in school. Still, I worried.

A week later, I was walking on a street near my son's
school when I saw my son and his teacher coming toward
me. They greeted me with brief hellos and passed on.
That evening I asked my son where the two of them had
been going.

"Oh, she was taking me to lunch to talk about my emotional problems," he answered.

I felt my face grow hot with anger. Goddamn her! She
had ignored my letter. "What kind of nonsense is that!" I
burst out. "That's not her job. She's supposed to teach."

"She likes to talk about problems a lot. She's always getting
kids to discuss their feelings about their parents."

"Then she's out of line," I snapped, "and I intend to
report her."

"Don't do that," my son said with alarm. "She'll lose her
job. She's having a lot of trouble with her boyfriend, and
she doesn't have much money."

"Does she tell the class all *her* personal problems as well?"
I asked in astonishment.

He acknowledged that she did.

"Then she deserves to lose her job."

"Nobody will listen to you, anyway," was his final comment.

Secretly I agreed with him. Being listened to and taken seriously hadn't been a very large part of my past experience. My parents had been unhearing and unmoving, as had been most of the men in my life—a few women as well. I had spent too many exhausting and frustrating hours trying to make myself heard to feel that I could have real impact.

"Listen to me, please. Just hear my side," I would plead hysterically to my mother, trying to explain to her why I wanted to do something or why I didn't want to do something. "This is so important to me." No response: my mother's mouth thin and taut like a mail slot; her back stiff and unyielding.

Desperately I'd turn to my father: "Won't you listen to what I have to say? I have a right to be listened to."

My father would smile uncomfortably and tell me that he agreed with whatever my mother had decided.

"Won't somebody listen?" I'd cry to the air. "Won't somebody listen?" I'd scream, pulling at my dress, wanting to rip it to shreds.

"You're getting hysterical," my mother would say reprovingly, and she and my father would leave the room.

I was sure the director of the school would be equally unhearing. He'd label me a hysterical parent, a busybody, a meddler. He'll think I'm jealous of the teacher because my son likes her, I cautioned myself. Was I jealous of her? No, I didn't think I was. I was truly concerned about her behavior in the classroom.

To my absolute surprise, the director of the school showed

equal concern. He said he hadn't been aware of the discussion of problems in the classroom and assured me that such a practice was not sanctioned by the school. He would definitely look into the matter. He would definitely put a stop to any amateur psychiatry that was going on. He thanked me for calling. *He thanked me!*

The following week my son informed me that his teacher wasn't talking to him, and it was all my fault.

"Has she been unkind to you?" I asked, ready to do battle again now that I knew attention would be paid.

"No. She just doesn't talk to me in the old way." He looked at me with something between annoyance and admiration. "You're getting to be a real troublemaker."

I smiled sweetly. "I do hope so," I said in my most pleasant voice. "And about time, too."

My final resolution—not to rush headlong into a relationship—was put to the test on snowy January 1, 1976. On that day I went to brunch where I was the lone single woman among five couples and one single man. I was the last to arrive, and as I walked into the room I saw the single man's eyes light up. I began to glow a little myself; perhaps a new romance was in the offing.

The man, whose name was Steve, and I had very little conversation during the early part of the afternoon. We sat on opposite sides of the room, engaged in separate conversations. But that didn't prevent us from directing "meaningful" glances toward one another every few minutes.

Later in the afternoon, Steve came over and sat next to me on the couch. Looking out the window at the falling snow, he whispered seductively that ideally at this moment we two should be lying next to each other on a sunny beach in the Virgin Islands. Instinctively I started to go along with the fantasy. I saw us sexy and tanned, our sleek, oiled bodies entwined, kissing passionately with sun-warmed lips. Fortunately—or unfortunately, depending on your point of view—as I began to answer him in a sultry contralto (my speciality, a different octave for every occasion), I heard that inner voice of reason:

What are you starting? You don't even know this man and already you're halfway in bed with him. And he doesn't even know you and he's dreaming his dreams. For once, take your time. Play it straight. Enough of the games. The results are always the same: disappointing and painful and time-wasting.

I sighed. It had been three and a half months without a man. Who knew when another would come along? Yet I'd been doing pretty well since I'd broken up with Josh. I didn't have that old clutchy, needy feeling anymore. But oh it was so tempting to waft into the clouds on wings of romance. And yet, hadn't I wafted with Stuart, Andrew, and Josh, and each time hadn't I come down to earth with a terrible crash? Maybe it *would* be a good idea to keep my feet on the ground right from the start. I sighed again, turned to Steve, and said apologetically:

"I really don't much like lying in the sun. I'm allergic to the sun."

"Oh, well," he continued sotto voce, still determined to make us a picture-book couple. "We can ski down mountain slopes together."

I braced myself. "I don't ski."

He seemed disappointed. "What do you do?"

"I love to walk. I adore walking on the beach when it's not too hot. I like to walk in the mountains."

He replied that walking wasn't his thing.

"I swim and do yoga," I added hopefully.

He didn't seem too impressed with those revelations either, but nevertheless edged a little closer and remarked that no doubt we were both just about the same age.

I took a good look at him. His hair, beard, and moustache were flecked with gray. We did appear to be the same age.

Yet somehow, I suspected he might be younger than I—perhaps by five or six years.

"I think I'm older than you are," I replied, feeling virtuous at being so honest.

"I'm thirty-five," he said. "How old are you?"

I gulped and paled. I knew very well how old I was. I had just turned forty-eight the day before. I had thirteen years on him. Should I lie?

To what purpose? asked my rational self.

So he'll continue to be interested in me.

I thought you were going to be straight.

You're right. I wanted to cry.

"I'm forty-eight," I said to Steve, seeing my last chance for happiness going up in smoke. "My birthday was yesterday."

Now it was his turn to gulp and pale. "Happy birthday," he said faintly.

"Thanks."

"Well," he continued gallantly—or maybe truthfully—"I've always liked older women."

We both laughed. End of fantasy. From then on, our conversation was straightforward. I listened to the tale of his divorce, his kids, his work, and I told him about myself. He was nice; I was nice. We were two pleasant middle-aged people (What was that about sleek, oiled bodies? Ahem!) with all sorts of conflicting ideas and problems. A few days later we had dinner together. And that was it. Without the patina of excitement, we found we had little in common. Neither of us was much interested in pursuing the relationship further.

Look what you've done to me, I railed at my rational self. You've condemned me to more solitary Saturday nights.

You don't need Steve. You can go out as much as you want. Besides, you did a lot of going out with Andrew and Josh, and where did it get you? And you had a very active social life with your husband. Would you like to comment on those seventeen years?

Okay! Okay! Truce. I don't really want to settle for trappings. I do want something more. Why not? I finished boldly. I deserve it.

Ah, replied my rational self. Now you're talking.

Chapter VII

I somehow expect my son to fail, just as I expect to fail. Why should I expect that? Whom would that spite? Or do I actually think of my son as an extension of myself, and then his failure is my failure? That sounds more like it. I must get rid of that notion before I do too much damage.
—From my journal, March 15, 1966

Although I was asserting myself boldly on several fronts, I was still wrestling uneasily with mother-son problems. Much of the battle was in my head. One part of me wanted everything ordered and neat: my son should be polite and helpful; he must not do anything to make me anxious; his activities and friends should all meet with my approval; I expected him to be an enthusiastic and conscientious student.

The other part of me was trying to look at him exactly as he was. Yes, it was important that he be polite and helpful, but given the many years of letting him walk all over me, it was unlikely he would quickly evolve into a model son —and was a model son even possible? Or desirable? Moreover, as a teen-ager, he was going through physical and emotional changes that often made him moody, angry, and frustrated—simply trying to manipulate a cracked voice that had once been a clear soprano was proving to be a difficult adjustment. He had his own problems, and I had to respect them.

And he wasn't about to construct his life around my anxieties, especially since my anxieties were always irrational. As an example, I can recall one humid night in the summer of 1976 when my son was off to a rock concert in Central Park. I had felt perfectly comfortable about his going until a woman, who was having supper at my house, began to speak nervously and vividly of her teen-aged son's terror of being mugged. On and on she talked, her voice rising in hysteria. I could feel my scalp begin to crawl, while an invisible band tightened across my chest. Would my son get home safely that night? Who knew what dangers lay in wait for him in the dimly lit park or on the teeming New York streets? I spent the remainder of my friend's visit beset by images of violence with my son as a helpless victim. And all the while, that oppressive band kept tightening across my chest.

By the time the woman left, I was a wreck. Where was my son? It was getting late. I wanted him home, safe in his room. I opened the front door, listened to hear if the elevator was coming up. No sound. Oh, God! Why wouldn't that band loosen? *Where was he?*

I went into the living room and sat in my rocking chair and tried to get my panic under control. What was going on with me? Why had I suddenly become so frightened? What had made me see my son as this vulnerable creature, prey to attack from all sides? I knew very well that he was a street-wise kid (unlike my friend's son); he had spent his entire fourteen-and-a-half years in New York City and was very adept at avoiding trouble. Did I want to wrap him in cotton and lock him in his room so I'd never have to worry? What kind of nonsense was that?

And then I remembered that my mother had wanted to keep me in a cocoon when I was young. Whenever I did anything unfamiliar, she'd become frantic with anxiety. And her fears were so bizarre; if I went out with a boy who wasn't Jewish, she'd go through all kinds of hand-wringing anguish. Her concern had nothing to do with religious beliefs, since religion had been almost non-existent in my upbringing. Her fear revolved around the possibility that should the boy and I have a fight he would call me a "dirty Jew"— an epithet, she was convinced, that had the power to strike me dead.

During a summer vacation from high school, while I prepared to go off to the San Joaquin Valley to pick grapes, my mother hovered over me, ominously predicting that I would be felled by a mysterious malady called "valley fever." Years later, as I packed to return to New York from Los Angeles, my mother had an anxiety attack because I was taking a jar of Farmer's Market homemade peanut butter back to my husband—"I'm sure it will explode when you reach a high altitude," she had worried aloud in a voice of doom.

Oh, how I had laughed at her fears. But ultimately the laugh was on me—unconsciously, I had absorbed them. Through the years, those anxieties had clung to me like so many leeches. I had spent my life trying to shake them off, but they were shake-resistant. Exorcism was required, not a mere shaking. Now, in the grand old family tradition, I was no doubt passing them on to my son. Terrific, I thought dryly, just what he needs.

But wait! Wasn't there a parallel? I had reacted to my friend exactly as I had reacted to my mother. I had incorporated her fears and the fears of her son as though they applied to me and my son. But they didn't, no more than my mother's anxieties had ever had any relevance to my reality.

Ah! What a relief! That last thought had caused the band across my chest to loosen. Obviously, I had hit on the truth. What a blessed freedom! I could breathe again! Of course my son would get home safely. He always had in the past. Sure, there were possibilities of danger; that was part of living. But I couldn't demand that he immobilize himself so that my life be tranquil. He had to be free to test the world out there, and I would have to cope with those inherited fears alone.

Another area of conflict was my son's choice of activities. I was trying to push him into what I considered acceptable pursuits, while he was determined to find his own interests. Instead of respecting his judgment and his ability to learn from experience, I was positive he would make enormous mistakes unless he had the benefit of my great wisdom. Therefore, I was a constant Greek chorus: everything he did, every question asked or statement made earned him a lecture, an evaluation, a judgment. As I strove to raise my self-esteem as an indispensable giver of advice, I was hacking away at my son's ego by completely disregarding any of his ideas and opinions. Talking to me, or trying to extract my approval, was like dealing with vapor.

One afternoon during that same summer, I walked outside my apartment house and saw a group of young people congregated across the street. Automatically, I started making comparisons (shades of my mother): what a nice, wholesome group of kids; how lovely to see them out in the air, tossing a Frisbee, sharing some laughs. Why wasn't my son with them? Why did he insist on remaining in his air-conditioned room? (Perhaps because it was ninety degrees out in the air.) Why did he have to make model airplanes all by himself, rather than becoming part of a group? Why did he have to be different?

Fortunately for my son, this time he was spared the usual lecture by the intervention of my rational self: What makes you think the other kids are better than your son?

They look better, I answered defensively. They're in a group. They're not alone in their rooms. It's not right to sit alone.

Look who's talking, snapped back my rational self. *You* sit alone. Why can't your son have the same privilege? Besides, he can't win with you; when he's with other kids, you still find fault.

Reluctantly, I admitted that was so. I was always mistrustful of his friends. What did I know of them? All those Sams

and Eds and Toms and Nancys and Janes he met in the park.
Who knew what shady things they were involved in, what
drugs they were smoking or swallowing or sniffing?

Oh, for heaven's sake, countered my rational self, you always have visions of nefarious types, and when the kids
come to your house they turn out to be middle-class boys
and girls just like your son. And even if they weren't as
clean-cut as you might like, they're your son's friends, not
yours. He has to make his own decisions about them.

Yes, it was all true, and still I was a network of suspicions.
I snooped, I listened, I sniffed the air for marijuana. I imagined the worst. It was wearing and wearying; it kept my son
continually in my orbit.

My therapist observed that I was much too involved in
my son's life. "It sounds as though you don't have enough
in your own life," she said.

I acknowledged that might be so.

"You have to separate yourself from him," she continued.
"For your sake, as well as his. It's important you concentrate
on your own goals. I realize you're terrified that if you don't
control all his actions they'll get out of hand, and then
you'll be called on to make things magically right—just as
you were called on by your parents. But it doesn't have to
be that way. Your son can learn to deal with the consequences of his actions. In fact, it's vital that he does learn.
And you must learn that you have value, even when you're
not there to give advice and to put everything back in
order."

Using supreme self-control, I did manage to ease up a bit
for the remainder of the summer. I tackled my own work
with vigor and valiantly refrained from making daily un-
favorable comments about model building and kids who
hang out in the park "doing nothing." When friends visited
my son, I forced myself to walk quickly past his closed door
without straining to pick up scraps of conversation. I must
confess, however, that I was not always able to control my

nose; it continued to sniff the air for evidence of the "dread weed." I'd sigh with relief when no fumes assailed my delicate nostrils—months later I discovered that the reason I never smelled anything was because the kids were smoking their joints out the window.

When school started, I fell back on my old tricks. I badgered my son about getting up in the morning and going to bed at night. I pushed him to do homework, to read more, to watch television less. His angry outbursts, which had subsided in the past months, started up again. But now I could see that I had a hand in causing them. I was driving him crazy. I wouldn't leave him alone. What else could he do but strike out at me?

So once more I attempted to retreat. Let him handle his homework, I admonished myself. The worst that could happen is that he'll flunk a subject and have to take it over. That's not so terrible. In fact, if memory serves, you had to repeat a couple of courses during your school days. Those were good experiences; they strengthened you.

It was a trying period. I picked my cuticles raw in an effort to keep my mouth shut about homework, bedtime, and waking time. When my son slept through the alarm two mornings in a row, I commanded myself to *stay out of it.* Both times I refrained from knocking on his bedroom door or calling out cheerily to "rise and shine." But I couldn't stop myself from clumping past his room in heavy shoes, talking loudly on the phone, or playing the radio at a high-decibel level. A lot of good it did. My son, who claimed he woke at the drop of a pin during the night, managed to sleep blissfully through all the morning commotion.

Thank goodness, the school stepped in. They warned my son that coming late or missing a class would be reflected in his grades—a far more persuasive argument than my repeated urgings to "get up and meet the day."

All was not resolved, however. There were plenty more late days and missed days, but I could choose to be out of it. Truthfully, I didn't always choose. Habit kept drawing me back into the fray. Also, when I wasn't involved, I'd feel left out, abandoned: if he and the school could get on without me, did that mean I had no importance? Was there no one who needed me and wanted me? And once again I'd point out to myself that my son was entitled to make his own way, and I'd have to find my self-esteem in my own work. It was one of my hardest struggles.

I went through similar conflicts in regard to homework. I wouldn't say anything to my son, but I'd listen at his door for evidence of work being done. Oh, Lord! He's on the phone again! Then I'd sit nervously in the living room, picking at my nails, arguing with myself about the advisability of reminding him that he should study for his math test or get started on his history paper. Sometimes the pull to interfere would become too great and I'd go into my anxious-mother act, but little by little restraint began to triumph.

The result was that there were a lot of late papers—a few never done at all—and plenty of tests taken that showed lack of preparation. But at least I was allowing some space for my son to make his own decisions about his education. Two years later, when he was again becoming sloppy toward the schoolwork, I was strong enough to offer him the option of dropping out—"The way you're approaching school," I said, "you might as well drop out." It was a tempting offer. But after considerable thought, and with no pressure from me, he made a decision in favor of a stronger commitment to his education. It was a turning point for both of us.

Another turning point for me came about through a most innocuous event—the purchase of a chair. It started this way; in the fall of 1976, my son mentioned that the bentwood desk chair in his room was falling apart. He needed a new one. "Fine," I replied, although I felt the usual knot in my stomach at the prospect of having to spend money.

My son then informed me that he wanted a high-back,

leather executive chair. He showed me a picture from the *New Yorker* magazine of the one he coveted—a little five-hundred-dollar job.

I laughed. He was making a joke.

No, he wasn't, he declared. He was completely serious.

"Out of the question," I told him. It was absurd for a boy his age to have such a grand chair. In addition, I couldn't possibly afford it. A nice fifty-dollar straight chair would be quite adequate. I'd get him a throw pillow for the seat if he needed it.

No way! He wanted an executive chair.

For several months we went back and forth on the chair affair. "How about one of those cushioned secretarial chairs?" I finally suggested, feeling magnanimous.

No. He wanted something with arms and a high back.

"How about something with arms and a low back?"

No. He wanted a high back. And he wanted it to swivel and to tilt backwards.

"That's inappropriate for a teen-ager," I retorted with growing impatience.

He didn't care. That's what he wanted. He'd been stubborn in the past, but I'd never seen him this set on something. Nevertheless, I didn't see how I could possibly give in to such an unrealistic demand.

By early spring 1977, the bentwood chair had collapsed and my son was substituting a dining-room chair. As I watched him tilt back and forth on a piece of furniture that was never meant to be tilted on, I decided the purchase of a new chair was an absolute necessity. There was no point in getting another wooden chair; he'd just rock on it and break it as he had done with the bentwood, and as he might very well do with the dining-room chair. I could see he needed something more substantial. Maybe I could find a bargain.

So off I went to a furniture warehouse. The bargains were

atrocious: black vinyl monstrosities with heavy wooden frames. They weren't even comfortable.

And then I saw *the* chair. Its arms and legs were of sleek chrome, and the seat and back—yes, a high back— were covered in a handsome woven fabric. And it tilted and swiveled. When I sat down, the back of the chair seemed to curve to fit my spine. Heavenly!

"How much?" I asked the salesman.

"One hundred eighty-five," he replied.

I felt a new knot form in my stomach. I knew that wasn't a huge amount for a good chair—a lot better than five hundred dollars—but I had figured on spending no more than one hundred dollars. Still, it was such a terrific chair, maybe I should go the extra eighty-five dollars. But for a teen-ager?

"It's really inappropriate for a teen-ager, isn't it?" I queried the salesman almost apologetically.

"How old is he?" he asked.

"Fifteen." I felt so embarrassed. Such an indulgence for a fifteen-year-old.

"How tall is he?"

"As tall as I am. Five-feet-seven or eight." What puzzling questions.

"He's tall," the salesman commented. "In a year it's likely he'll be quite tall. He'll need a big chair."

I was dumbfounded. He was doing something I hadn't even thought of; he was looking at my son as an individual, rather than as just another teen-ager.

"How many other chairs does he have in his room?" was his next question.

"Oh, my goodness!" I replied, my eyes wide with amazement. "It never occurred to me that his desk chair is his only chair. He uses it for everything: homework, reading, TV watching, listening to music. Friends visit him in his room so he needs something other than his bed to sit on. And he doesn't have a carpet on the floor so it's not too good for sitting. A little wooden chair probably isn't very adequate for his needs."

"It sounds like this is the perfect chair for him," remarked the salesman. "It's a very solid chair. It will last him for years. I have one just like it myself, and I'm crazy about it. Your son can use it in college."

He was absolutely right. It was the perfect chair for this particular boy, with his particular room and his particular needs. And I had never even realized it. It took a stranger to show me how to look at my son as a special, unique person. With shaking hands I wrote a check for $185 plus tax and went home in a daze.

My son loved the chair. It was even better than the one in the magazine. It was, and still is, and will continue to be for a long time—perfect!

Workshop IV

"Hey, Julia, where were you last week?" Laura's question starts off the session.

"We missed you," Ann adds.

Julia blushes. It is evident she is embarrassed. "I did a dumb thing!" she exclaims, shaking her head in exasperation.

Six pairs of eyes focus on her. I ask what she did that was so dumb. Julia pauses, takes a deep breath, and says: "You remember the man I told you about a few weeks ago, the one who never wants to get together on weekends?"

Everyone nods. Connie wants to know if he's the one who sees his children on weekends. Julia grimaces and replies that he is. She continues:

"Late last Thursday afternoon he called me at the office and said he had a free evening and he wanted to see me. Could he come by after work? That made me very confused: I was so happy he had called, but yet I didn't want to miss the workshop. I reminded him that I had the workshop and said I really hated skipping a session and could we get together afterwards. I was hoping he'd make it easy for me but he didn't. He said afterwards was kind of late—he wanted an early evening. When I couldn't make up my mind, he got annoyed and said that I'm always pushing at him to see me more, and now that he wanted to see me I was telling him no. He was getting tired of mixed messages. That made me feel really guilty, so I said okay he could come by. I told him I'd cook him dinner." Julia again gives a disgusted shake of her head. "What a jerk I am," she states vehemently.

Connie observes that we've all done exactly the same thing at one time or another; if a man calls we usually cancel everything, including dates with our women friends, no matter how important they are to us.

"Did you at least have a good time with him?" Elaine wonders.

"No! It was rotten!" Julia bursts out. "I cooked him dinner, which I didn't want to do, and then we sat up until three in the morning talking about our 'relationship.'"

"I thought he didn't want to have a late evening," Ann interjects sarcastically.

Julia makes another face: "I thought so, too. Anyhow, we talked for hours about where our relationship was going and all that stuff. I kept pushing for some kind of commitment, and he kept repeating that he had this block against making a commitment." Her lip curls at the word "block." "It was a big waste of time, and I ended up being furious at myself for not going to the workshop." She looks at us sadly. "I hope I didn't miss too much. Sometimes I can be sooo . . . dumb!"

Ann comments that Julia shouldn't be angry at herself, that she had no way of knowing it was going to turn out to be an awful evening.

Julia replies that she knew from the start it was a mistake, and that she hadn't followed her instincts.

"Why do women always do that?" Laura asks. "Men never give up things when women want to see them."

"That's for sure," states Julia.

I remark that I don't like dealing in generalities, but it's pretty true that women in our culture have traditionally felt they had to attach themselves to a man in order to be a complete human being. Therefore, no activity, no interest, could possibly be important enough to take precedence over a "relationship." Men, on the other hand, usually get their self-esteem from their work, or the amount of money they earn, or their various activities—sports, etc.

"Fortunately," I add, "the feminist movement has changed a lot of the old thinking. Women today take their abilities and their interests much more seriously; they're less ready to throw everything aside for a man. But despite all the advances, many of us are still prey to all those ingrained feelings of inadequacy and incompleteness when we're not part of a couple. Our job now is to work on ourselves until we can feel whole and complete whether we have a man in our lives or not."

"So how do you do that?" Laura asks insistently.

I say that the one thing we can do is to work at trying to stop the old automatic behavior: we can go back to how we were brought up to believe that our survival depended on keeping a man in our orbit; then we can become aware that hanging on to a man can actually be destructive. I point to Julia as an example: she had wanted to come to the workshop; she had felt it had value for her; yet she had put it aside when "Mr. Right" had called.

"He's hardly 'Mr. Right,'" Julia comments bitterly.

I tell her that I was being facetious. "The truth is," I continue, "'Mr. Right' is a myth. Most of us know that intellectually, but emotionally we still believe in it."

Julia states wearily that she doesn't know how you ever get over believing in it.

I acknowledge that it's hard, but I remind her that, as I mentioned in the second session, it helps to listen to the other person. That way she can see where he's coming from. She'll realize that he's not Superman, that he's a simple human being like she is. Then she can ask herself what she can realistically expect from him in a relationship. And she has to listen to *herself*; she has to take her evaluations and her needs seriously. "Which is exactly what you didn't do. You told us that you knew from the start how things would work out, yet you ignored your own very good judgment."

Susan cuts in: "I know why she ignored her judgment. She was afraid if she refused him he'd stop seeing her altogether. Isn't that right, Julia?"

Julia nods.

"Every time you describe him, I get the feeling you'd be better off without him," observes Connie. "He sounds like an insensitive creep."

Julia replies that she doesn't know why she hangs on to him.

My suggestion is that she try to understand her reasons. She could ask herself what she gets from the relationship. How does it compare with past relationships? What are the negative aspects of the relationship? Can she be an independent person with this man, or does he demand she be available whenever he calls? Does she want that? Does this man give value to her goals, or does he disregard them? Is she satisfied with the trade-offs?

As I go through the list of questions, Julia groans, evoking laughter from the other women.

I laugh, too, and tell her I'm sympathetic with her groans. But the only way she'll be able to make any kind of decision is by understanding why she's in the relationship, what's going on with her and the man, and what her options are.

"Oh, damn!" Julia exclaims. "Why is everything so hard? I don't know what I feel about him. But I do know it's a big relief not to have to plan my social life. It's true the weekends are left open, but at least I can rely on having two nights in the middle of the week taken care of. The thought of having to start calling people and planning things makes me want to scream."

"Me, too," Laura declares firmly. "Having to plan your own social life is the worst part of being single."

Suddenly everyone is talking at once. They have strong feelings on the subject. Each cites an example of how she can't bear taking responsibility for creating a social life.

"When you're married," states Julia, "you always know you have a person to do things with. You don't have to worry about holidays or weekends." She sighs deeply. "Sundays are the worst."

Laura and Connie concur that Thanksgiving is the most difficult day to deal with; both get very upset if they're not invited to a typical family dinner. Elaine mentions that with her daughter gone and her husband so remote she dreads Christmas. Susan remarks that she's never had to make any arrangements for her social life because she's always had a husband or a boyfriend. "I don't think I'd know how to begin," she concludes helplessly.

I point out that part of the problem comes from the notion that those days must be *filled*, that one must *do* something. If you think in terms of what you want to do—if, in fact, you want to do anything at all—you have much less of a problem.

"For example," I explain, "if you believe that Sundays are family days, or going-to-brunch days, or being-with-a-special-someone days, then you're operating on a superficial level; you're going to get really hung up if you don't have a family or a person to go to brunch with, or a special someone to be with. The same holds true when you view holidays in conventional terms; if you assume they should be loving, wonderful, family days, and you don't happen to have a loving, wonderful family, you're going to feel wretched. But if you look at all days in terms of how, within the framework of your life-style, you can best enjoy them, you'll be much more comfortable about making plans. Sunday doesn't have to be anything more than what you want it to be. You don't have to sit around a Thanksgiving table with a huge family for the day to be pleasant—let's face it, only too often that huge family turns out to be a huge drag. In the long run, it's far better to carve out your own pleasures than to wait for someone else to do it for you, or to slavishly follow conventions. How many times have you followed conventions? How many times have you let others decide the way an evening or a day or a vacation should be spent? And how many times have you been disappointed and resentful?"

I seem to have struck a chord, for I see six heads incline thoughtfully and affirmatively.

At this point Connie interrupts and tells us she had an experience that "sort of illustrates" what we're talking about. She relates that last Friday she had "this big impulse" to celebrate her transfer to the new department but couldn't find anyone who was free to celebrate with her, or who could afford to.

"I wanted to go *that* evening to an elegant French restaurant," she says, "and I wanted to have a fabulous, expensive meal with lots of wine. I was so disappointed that none of my friends was available. I had pretty much decided to put it off, or not to go at all, when I remembered our discussion about eating alone. I thought: 'I really want to go tonight. I don't want to put it off. So what the hell! I'll celebrate by myself.' Before I could lose my nerve, I phoned the restaurant and made a reservation. That night I put on some pretty clothes and I went." She smiles at us triumphantly.

"Were you nervous?" Susan wonders. I get the impression that she's nervous just thinking about it.

"Yeah. I really was," Connie recalls. "But it turned out to be a fantastic evening. I had a great time."

The women look at Connie with admiration. They're definitely impressed with her independence.

"Didn't you feel at all lonesome celebrating by yourself?" Julia asks.

Connie replies that she had been afraid of being depressed, but the restaurant had turned out to be so nice, the waiters so pleasant, and the food and wine so good that she couldn't help enjoying herself.

"I'm going to do it again," she promises. "Now that I've

broken the ice, I can try all sorts of restaurants without feeling uncomfortable. I will change one thing, though. Last Friday I was given a table way in the back. I didn't mind it because I liked being tucked away my first time out alone, but next time I'll ask for a front table."

I observe that she's right when she says her experience illustrates what we were talking about. If she had followed the convention that claims you have to celebrate with someone, or if she hadn't been willing to make plans and arrangements, she would have missed a lovely evening.

"How long did you sit all alone?" Julia asks. Every time Julia utters the word "alone," her voice conjures up an image of someone in solitary confinement on a diet of bread and water.

"Gee, I don't know," Connie replies. "I didn't feel I had to rush. I took my time: I drank a few toasts to myself, I sipped my wine, I looked around the room, I joked with the waiters. Maybe I was there around an hour and a half. I liked . . ."

She is interrupted by an announcement from Laura: "I did something alone, too," she says shyly.

We look at her with surprise. Only two weeks ago she had revealed her terror of doing anything by herself.

In response to our stares of amazement, Laura confides that she saw half a play by herself.

"Half a play!" Ann exclaims. "What happened to the other half?"

Laura smiles, begins to twist a frizzy curl, and says timidly: "Well, I went to the play with my friend, and we were sitting together up in the balcony. But when intermission came, my friend wanted to move down to some empty seats in the orchestra. I didn't want to move. I didn't want to take a chance of being thrown out of the orchestra. Besides," she adds defensively, "I was happy where I was. So she went downstairs, and I stayed up in the balcony and watched the second half of the play alone." She looks pleased and embarrassed. "It wasn't bad at all. In fact, it was kind of fun."

Ann says: "I think you're terrific, Laura. Congratulations on the big step."

The other women echo her.

"Do you think next time you'll be able to see a whole play alone?" Elaine asks.

Laura shrugs. "Maybe," she answers, "but I'm not promising anything. Greta said you should go slowly and not make big demands on yourself, and that's what I'm doing."

Everyone agrees that's a good idea. There are a few more encouraging words for Laura, and then the women return to the subject of holidays. How *does* one handle them when there's not a ready-made family?

Ann mentions that her network of friends serves as a substitute family. There are always festive communal gatherings at Thanksgiving, Christmas, and New Year's Eve.

"But what do you do if you don't have a group of friends?" Laura wonders.

I say that I know people who make a point of not celebrating holidays at all.

"I'd hate that," Ann responds.

"I'm not advocating that everyone ignore holidays," I hasten to reply. "I only wanted to illustrate that you can do what you want. In my case, I try to base my holiday plans on how things are going between my son and myself, how I'm feeling at that particular time, how much money I have—very important—and what kind of celebration my son is looking forward to. That approach seems to work best for me."

Julia's way is to try and re-create the holidays she had when her husband was alive and her kids were younger. "Only it never works," she comments sourly. "The kids really want to be with their friends, and my son always wants to go skiing. They couldn't care less about family dinners. I tell them they have a responsibility to me; it's not fair to leave me alone at holidays."

Predictably, Elaine firmly endorses Julia's point of view. "They're your only family. They should be with you at holidays."

I tell her I don't agree. "Why should things be forced when there might be happier alternatives?"

"What alternatives could there possibly be?" Elaine asks belligerently.

"One alternative could be that Julia could go skiing herself—not with her son, of course. Or she could go to a resort, or out to dinner with a friend." I turn to Julia. "If you keep trying to imitate the past, you don't leave any room for being creative in the present. You have a new life. Why not explore its possibilities, rather than clutching at the old life?"

"I didn't choose the new life," Julia answers stubbornly.

"You may not have chosen it, but you *have* it. And you do have a choice: you can fight it forever; or you can accept it and make something good of it. If I were you, I'd go with the latter. It's bound to give you a lot more pleasure than the fruitless course you've been pursuing."

No reply from Julia. I do hope she doesn't feel I've been dumping on her all night. She certainly has been the recipient of a lot of advice from all of us. On the other hand, everything we've said has been out of concern for her. No one has wanted to put her down.

My thoughts are interrupted by Elaine, who remarks that she doesn't see how you can deviate from tradition without becoming depressed. I respond that if decisions are made by consulting one's own needs and one's specific situation, there's usually nothing to be depressed about. I immediately add that I don't mean to make it all sound easy as pie. I tell the women that I've gotten plenty depressed in my time, but I can usually come out of it by focusing in on some concrete things I want to do. If I keep looking around enviously, or trying to follow tradition or an accepted formula, I only get more depressed. But when I start to look for alternatives that will work for me, I can feel myself come alive again.

Connie breaks in to say that she couldn't agree with me more, and I comment that her going to a restaurant alone is a good illustration of the point I'm trying to make. I address the whole group: "Connie wanted to celebrate her new job and she wanted to do it on a particular night, in a particular way. She could very well have sat around moaning about the fact that there was no one to go with, that no one loved her, that other people had someone to celebrate with and she didn't. And very soon she would have been feeling terribly sorry for herself. Instead, she sized up the possibilities, made a decision within the possibilities, and carried it out. And she had a wonderful time. Here's another example: just recently my son said to me that we have a perfect relationship. And at that moment I realized it *was* perfect—for us. However, another family would probably hate our arrangement, would find it really depressing. What has happened is that over the past five years we've developed a life-style that reflects our needs, our personalities, and the limitations of our situation. And it has very little to do with tradition or convention. When I was trying to make us live according to stereotypes, I was miserable. I was always comparing and wishing things were different. And my son was so resentful. Now we've achieved a degree of harmony. That only happened because I was willing to try something a little different."

The women then ask for concrete suggestions on coping with holidays.

"As far as I'm concerned, anything goes," I tell them. "Thanksgiving could involve a turkey for two at home, or eating at a Chinese or French restaurant with a friend, or having a big communal dinner, or going on a hiking trip or to a yoga retreat. It's fun to approach it without rules. Then you're free to choose whatever suits you. You can do the same with Christmas and New Year's Eve. The main thing to remember is not to leave things to chance or other people. Make it your business to decide what *you* want to do— even if your decision is to do nothing. If you're making the choices, the chances are you won't feel abandoned and bereft. In fact," I conclude, "this takes us back to what we were talking about earlier—the importance of taking responsibility for planning your own life. The more you do it in all areas, the better you'll feel about yourself."

Susan comments that planning activities for oneself takes money. Therefore, she allows her boyfriend to make most of their plans since he's the one with the larger income. That leads Julia to ask the other women what they do about handling money when they go on dates. Do they let the man pay? Do they pay for themselves?

"I always expect my boyfriend to pay," Laura answers. Then, bitterly: "The one thing he has to offer is money."

"Sometimes the man pays, sometimes not," Ann says.

"When does he pay and when not?" is Julia's next question. "How do you decide?"

"Let's say a new man invites me to dinner," Ann explains. "Then I figure he should pay; he's taking me out so we can get acquainted—it's his party. But if I'm going with someone for awhile, and he's not making much more money than I am, we'll usually work out plans together and we'll split the bill."

My advice is to go by individual needs, as Ann seems to do, rather than by rules. I mention one couple I know that has an arrangement whereby he pays when they go out and she pays for any entertaining at home. That seems to work for them. With another couple, the woman almost always pays; she makes twice as much as he does, and he's paying alimony and child support. "In my own case," I continue, "the majority of the men I become involved with make considerably more money than I. So if we decide to go somewhere expensive, it's with the understanding that I can't afford to contribute financially. But if it's something I can afford, I like the idea of splitting the cost. There are times, if I feel I can manage it, I'll even treat."

Elaine says she can't imagine what it would be like to start dating again. She dreads the whole idea.

"It's awful," Julia declares.

"I don't think it's so awful," is Ann's opinion. "It's nice to go out with different men. And it doesn't always have to be romantic."

I agree with her on that.

"Has anyone here ever taken the initiative in a relationship?" Julia asks. Her gaze goes around the circle. "Has anyone ever called a man for the first date?"

We all shake our heads no, and Julia asks why not? Why aren't we women more comfortable about calling men for dates?

Laura points out that our society has always frowned on women being aggressive, and she can't help being influenced by that viewpoint.

"I feel the same way," Susan says.

Connie's reason is that she's never had to make the first move, that men have always called her. But she also acknowledges that she would be uncomfortable in an aggressive role.

I tell them that I haven't made the first move with a man because I was brought up to wait for others to come to me—women as well as men. "However," I add, "I have changed a great deal in these past five years, and I do think I would be willing to call a man I don't know too well if I were interested in getting to know him better. Unfortunately, I haven't met anyone recently to whom I've felt particularly drawn."

All the women concur that meeting someone "simpatico" is the eternal problem. We sigh deeply in unison. The next minute we are laughing in unison at our collective wistfulness.

When our laughter subsides, I tell the women that since we've had some discussion about relationships tonight, if it's all right with them I'd like to conclude the session with a presentation of a code of ethics that could apply to relationships. Six blank stares indicate that none of them understands what I'm talking about.

I explain that recently I interviewed my therapist in connection with an article I was writing on marriage. During the interview she suggested that married people, or people in close relationships, really need to observe some kind of code of ethics with each other. Her feeling was that as soon as we enter a relationship, ethics go out the window. She pointed out that we observe business ethics, ethics in religion, in education, and there's even an ethic among thieves. But nobody talks about the ethics of a relationship. She then outlined for me a few rules that could apply to husbands and wives, lovers, parents and children, and even to very close friends. I ask the women if the subject interests them.

Yes, it does, they tell me.

"There are seven rules I'll talk about," I begin. "The first rule is not to cross the boundary line between you and the other person. To me that means that we have to recognize our separateness. And we have to respect it in ourselves and in others. No other person is an extension of us. We don't possess anyone, and no one possesses us. We all have a right to privacy, to space that won't be invaded.

"The second rule involves allowing the other person to be himself or herself. That means that we don't try to change someone; we don't put the other one down for being what he or she is. And we must demand the same respect for ourselves.

"Rule three: deciding for yourself what characteristics

in the other you can accept and what you cannot. That involves seeing the other clearly: thinking about the various qualities you like; what you don't like; and figuring out what the trade-offs are." I look at Julia. "That's what I was telling you to do in relation to the man you've been going with."

Julia replies that she had made the connection.

I continue: "The fourth rule emphasizes making it as clear as possible to yourself, as well as to the other person, exactly what's going on and what you're feeling. To do that you have to think very carefully before speaking and acting; you want to understand what your true motives are, and you want to be sure that you won't be sending out conflicting messages to the other person."

"Do you think I was giving out conflicting messages last Thursday?" Julia asks. "That's what my friend accused me of."

I reply that she *was* giving mixed messages, although there was no reason for him to treat it like a crime. She hadn't taken the time to decide for herself exactly what she wanted to do and why she wanted to do it; she had sort of hoped he'd be a good guy and get her off the hook. Actually, it was up to her to decide what her needs were for that night and then to spell them out to him very plainly.

"But I did tell him," Julia cuts in. "I told him I wanted to come to the workshop. I said I'd see him afterward."

"You said all that," I counter, "but you didn't really mean it. That's why it all came out as a mixed message. You weren't absolutely sure of what you felt and what you wanted—you sort of wanted it both ways—and so you couldn't be completely straight with him."

"But doing it your way would have involved his getting mad at me. Isn't that so?"

"Maybe. But things didn't work out too well your way, either. And you ended up feeling exploited and angry. So what was accomplished?"

"Not much," Julia answers.

I go on to rule number five. "That rule," I explain, "tells us not to have irrational expectations. In other words, we shouldn't expect a relationship to make our lives free of anxiety and trouble. Nor should we expect our children to behave as our parents. If we're involved with a remote man, it's irrational to expect him to be loving and sensitive and understanding. It's irrational to expect ourselves to be perfect or always available or completely in charge of everything that happens between us and the other person. As I said before, we have to view our relationships with unclouded vision.

"The sixth rule states that one should take responsibility for one's own decisions and behavior. Remember how I emphasized in our first session that we're not victims? That we make choices, even when we choose to do nothing? Well, we have to remind ourselves continually of that fact when we're in a relationship. How many times have you heard one spouse blame the other for his or her not being able to do something? Or how often have you heard a parent blame a child by saying: 'You made me hit you'? Putting the responsibility for your actions on someone else is unethical. The converse of that is that you're not responsible for the other person's actions.

"And finally, the seventh rule in this code of ethics is to be kind and civilized and respectful of each other."

I see that the women are startled by my last statement. "You all look surprised," I comment.

Ann reveals that she's very surprised. "That last rule is so obvious, and yet I never thought of it in terms of a relationship."

"I don't think it applies to a relationship," Laura declares. "Where else can you get out your anger and hostility if not with the people who are close to you?"

I say: "Why should we use people as our emotional and physical punching bags?"

"How else do you get anger out?" Laura persists.

"I don't believe the object should be simply to get the anger out. You have to use the techniques we've been talking about in these past weeks in order to understand why you get angry in the first place. And then you have to find ways of behaving differently so you don't get so angry. Dumping anger on your dear ones is no solution. In fact, it's very destructive."

Laura looks unconvinced, but Connie interrupts to remark that it's true that we're often kinder and more considerate to complete strangers than we are to people who are close to us.

"Exactly," I say. "We really take our relationships very much for granted. We have to learn to value and respect them. Having a code of ethics forces us to think about how we're behaving with our lovers and husbands and children, and how they're behaving with us. It helps us look at ourselves and them in a different light."

Our workshop ends shortly thereafter. Before we say goodnight, Susan reminds us that next week is our last session. The other women register sadness that the five weeks are almost over.

"If there are any topics we haven't touched on, bring them up next week," I tell them. "I'd like to cover as much as possible before we end." They agree to do so and we part.

I, too, am a bit sad as I walk up Madison Avenue. This has been an interesting and nice group of women, and I'll miss them.

And yet I know I'll see them again from time to time; no doubt we'll run into one another on the street or in a supermarket or on a bus. Only two weeks ago, on a subway, I had bumped into Sally, a forty-five-year-old divorced woman from my first workshop two years ago. In our brief conversation, she had reminded me of how dependent she had been on her ex-husband; she had automatically called him to fix things or to solve problems. "Now I do my own fixing and my own problem-solving," she had boasted. Then she had smiled shyly and added, "Your workshop helped push me in the right direction."

It had been a warming encounter. It had given me small evidence that the sessions can have some kind of lasting effect. The thought makes me smile, and a man coming toward me smiles seductively back. He thinks I'm flirting with him. I giggle to myself and pass him by.

Chapter VIII

I always think in terms of an audience. Even in my diary I don't reveal as much as I could. Maybe a few times when I'm caught up in something, but usually I'm thinking of the kind of impression I want to make. But that defeats the purpose of a diary. Let's face it! That's the way I live my life. It's got to stop!
—From my journal, November 18, 1959

It took almost five years after the separation from my husband before I was able to establish a life-style that was completely comfortable and right for me. I was so hooked into believing in a picture-book existence that it wasn't easy to abandon the stereotypes and to go by the realities of my own situation.

In the beginning, my feeling was that, because I had deprived my son of a nuclear family, I had an obligation to provide him with the trappings of a "warm family life." Therefore, although I couldn't stand the continual hubbub, I encouraged him to fill the house with his friends. Didn't lots of kids running in and out signify "happiness and cordiality?"

And, of course, I played my mother role to the hilt: I kept those "heavenly-smelling" pans of brownies and popovers coming out of the oven; a pot of Mother Walker's famous spaghetti sauce was frequently simmering on the stove; and I was alway ready to whip up "mouth-watering" cheeseburgers and hash-brown potatoes for a horde of hungry teen-agers.

During the married years, my son had been accustomed

to eating supper in his room in front of TV an hour before his father and I had our supper. But now I was determined to give him "real family dinners," where we two would sit at a candlelit table, eating nourishing, well-prepared meals, discussing the events of the day. To my surprise, my son wanted no part of it: he liked his solitary meals; he didn't want to miss his nightly viewing of "Star Trek"; he preferred TV dinners or a plate of pasta to my three-course repasts; he had absolutely no desire to talk over the happenings of the day with "dear old mom."

How humiliating! Could I tell my friends that my son didn't want to eat with me? How was I to face the world knowing that at suppertime my son gobbled food in front of television while I, a rejected figure, sat alone at our dining-room table?

I cajoled and pleaded for a united front, but it was a no-win situation. For even when I succeeded in luring my son into the dining room, his behavior was so sullen and resentful that I was always relieved when the last mouthful of dessert had been swallowed and we could leave the table and go our separate ways. Several times I followed my son's suggestion and joined him in his TV watching. But sitting in silence, balancing a plate on my knee, and watching the adventures of Captain Kirk and Mr. Spock hardly fit in with my concept of the ideal family dinner. Eventually I gave it up. Still, I had faith that somehow I would find a way to achieve the "togetherness" that would make our supper hour the memorable event I knew it should be.

My rational self often wondered why I was so intent on pursuing the dining-room scene. Didn't I realize that most often family dinners were far from ideal?

Sure enough, every time I'd recall those long-ago, sit-down suppers with mother, father, sister, and grandfather, I'd shudder. Talk about memorable: most conversations had ended in a fight, with either my sister or myself dashing from the table in tears. Some nights the radio would blare throughout the meal, and any attempts at communication would be met with a frown, a finger to the lips, and a loud "Sh!" Worst of all, everyone ate so fast; none of them ever paused for a breath, or a quiet chew, or simply to savor a wonderful taste. For my parents, meals were something to be gotten through. I saw them as competitions which I was always doomed to lose.

Your son eats the same way, my rational self usually commented. Aren't most meals with him pretty much like all those suppers of yore?

True, they were. But I believed they would change. My rational self remained skeptical.

As it turned out, I was the one to change. It started with my diet. After a couple of years, grains, vegetables, and beans became my favorite foods. My son wouldn't even taste them. Despite all my efforts to nourish him properly, he maintained his allegiance to junk food. Moreover, elaborate cooking had begun to bore me. I no longer saw myself as Saint Greta of the Kitchen every time I prepared a hearty three-course dinner. And since my son was gravitating toward spaghetti sauce from the jar—"A lot better than yours" —why in God's name was I knocking myself out over a hot stove? In fact, since both our meals were becoming last-minute concoctions, what was the point of making a big ceremony out of supper?

One night, after my son had gone off to his room with his dish of pasta, instead of going to my usual place at the dinner table, I took my plate of rice, beans, and vegetables into the living room and watched the news. The following night I did the same. Within a few months, I had established a routine.

It's only temporary, I told myself guiltily. Just until my son is ready to have supper with me.

But soon I had to admit that those chummy sit-down dinners I had always claimed I wanted were not what I craved now; maybe I had never really wanted them at all.

I liked our arrangement. My son liked it. So why was I fighting it?

When will we have warm mother-and-son conversations? I queried myself anxiously.

You have conversations all the time, was my reply. Although one could hardly describe them as "warm." You don't need a dining-room table and food in order to talk.

Isn't our arrangement strange?

Perhaps it is. Nevertheless, it seems to work for the two of you.

You know what's sad? I reflected. The fact that my son will never be able to tell people what a great cook his "mom" is.

What a tragedy! my rational self countered sarcastically. Let's hope you have more to offer than cooking.

I went through a similar pattern in regard to holidays. During 1974 and 1975, at least fifteen people sat down to my extended dining-room table for Thanksgiving dinners. I was trying to give my son a sense of community, of a surrogate family. But, with the exception of a cousin in his thirties and his wife, most of the guests were either friends of mine who my son knew only vaguely, or friends of my cousin's who neither my son nor I knew at all. (Close friends had their own family obligations and couldn't join us.) Although some people brought their children, there was very little interaction among them. For the most part, the kids sat shyly at the table waiting for the grownups to finish their festivities so they could go back to their familiar surroundings and their own friends.

In 1976, my son and I were invited to celebrate Thanksgiving with a family of six—mother, father, three sons, and a daughter. I accepted with delight. I had begun to weary of the big feasts in my house, and my son had confided that he hadn't much enjoyed the past celebrations with a bunch of strangers. The idea of being part of a warm, large family was very appealing. My son wasn't as thrilled as I. He didn't know the kids that well, he maintained. Whenever he'd been with them, they hadn't been all that friendly. After some prodding from me, however, he agreed it might be fun.

It was awful! Instead of participating in a scene of love and affection, my son and I found ourselves unwilling witnesses to the family's hostilities. We sat at the table virtually ignored while father continually leveled joking putdowns at mother; eighteen-year-old son interrupted everyone with his new-found college wisdom; and ten-year-old brother competed for equal time. The fifteen-year-old boy remained glum and silent. When the meal was coming to an end and we were sipping our coffee, the nine-year-old daughter, urged by her father, sat down to the piano (which was in the dining room) to practice a new piece she'd just learned. My son and I made an early escape.

Tradition be damned! The following year I asked my cousin and his wife to join my son and me for a simple repast for four. They declined in favor of a larger celebration. Other friends invited us to join them and their parents and uncles and cousins, so we wouldn't have to be without a family on this wonderful family day. No thanks, was my reply. Although it wasn't large, we did have a family—a family of two. We'd make do with that.

It worked out pretty well. In honor of the occasion, my son and I had dinner together. There weren't a dozen courses, so we didn't stagger from the table feeling bloated and sick. We ate our turkey and stuffing, cleared the table, washed the dishes (actually I washed the dishes), and then each did his and her "own thing." In 1978, my cousin and his wife decided to forgo the usual huge supper and to accept my invitation for dinner for four. We made it a communal effort and even tried some non-traditional dishes. After supper my son went off with friends, and my cousins and I sat around and talked. It was simple and pleasant. We declared it one of our better Thanksgivings. Perhaps next year we'd do the same, or maybe I'd feel like doing nothing.

I might even decide to have a large traditional dinner for a change. One thing was sure, the choice was mine.

It wasn't only suppers and holidays that were changing. I was going through a paring-down process in every area of my life.

I began to look at my clothes with a critical eye; so many of them had been bought to please my husband or to create an image—glamorous, sexy, up-to-date—rather than to reflect my taste and my life-style. For a long time I was unsure of my taste and the kind of life-style I wanted, but now I was getting clear about the fact that I felt comfortable in jeans, turtleneck sweaters, soft wool skirts, reefers, and blazers. My social life had become very simple; I never went anywhere that required "dressing up." So why was I hanging onto the fancy velvet evening jacket, the long skirts, the fur-trimmed coat that was too heavy and not really my style? Did I need the silver shoes? And what about that ersatz-silk tunic with its huge sleeves edged with long fringe? Whenever I wore it, that silly, loopy fringe caught on doorknobs and other people's buttons; it dripped into everything I ate. There were other items I had bought because they had been on sale or because I had allowed a salesperson to talk me into them: "It's what they're all wearing now. You look wonderful in it. You'll be right in style."

I piled clothes into shopping bags and sent them off to the thrift shop; I preferred a tax credit to a closet full of unworn outfits. I performed my task with such zeal that, when I finished, my wardrobe was pathetically sparse. For several months after, each time I'd open the closet my heart would sink; the emptiness seemed to serve as a metaphor for my entire life. I had done so much stripping away of old habits, behaviors, relationships, and activities that I wondered if I was doomed to an existence of unrelieved barrenness. Had I made some dreadful mistake with all my whittling away? Could I ever find or afford replacements?

If my closet was a metaphor, then the answer was yes.

Slowly, and with much anxiety, I began to buy new things that I loved and felt good in—always with the inevitable question: "Do I really need this?" (Often, in order to alleviate the guilt, I'd hold off getting something until I really *did* desperately need it. For example, I bought my reefer on a cold November day when I could no longer pretend that my unlined raincoat was sufficiently warm.) Sometimes I found bargains I liked, but more and more I was going for quality: a good pair of leather shoes that would hold up through my daily three-mile walks; a well-tailored blazer that would be in style for years to come. After many months, my closet had lost its spartan look. It was hardly opulent, but it no longer evoked feelings of depression and self-pity. The few carefully chosen pieces reflected a special person with special taste. It was a wardrobe I could build on.

Next came my apartment. One summer day in 1976, I glanced around and realized that very little in it had changed since my husband had moved out. I was still living with the clutter he had adored. Books, many unread, and records, many played only once, were piled high on shelves and on the floor in the living room, study, and foyer. Games and puzzles, some of them unopened, filled the foyer closet. Cupboards in the kitchen were bulging with fish tanks, snake and iguana cages, pumps, plastic plants, rocks, and filters. All relics of my husband's and son's days of animal collecting.

I wanted space! I wanted only *my* books, *my* records! I didn't want my home crammed with objects that had no relevance to my present life.

I filled thirty cartons with books and twenty cartons with records and called my ex-husband to come and get them. He had finally built his shelves and was happy to oblige. Once the cartons were gone, I emptied closets and kitchen cupboards and sent off more goodies to the thrift shop. It was exhilarating.

I was becoming aware that all my life I had lived in places that had nothing to do with my taste and my needs. When I was very young, I had shared a bedroom with my grandfather. My small bed had occupied a corner, while his oversized, heavy, veneered Grand Rapids dresser, chifforobe, and double bed had dominated all the rest of the available space. Later, I had bunked in with my sister and our live-in mother's helper. It was a cheerless, airless room. My sister had dozens of allergies, including dust, feathers, and night air. Thus, not a scrap of fabric could be used for decoration; pillows were verboten (those were pre-Dacron days), and all the windows were tightly sealed from dusk to dawn against the insidious night vapors.

In my junior year in college, I was finally given a room of my own. But there was the inevitable catch; my mother's frugality, and her need to control everything, prevented her from allowing me the freedom to furnish it exactly as I wanted. Moreover, the room wasn't totally mine. I could have it to myself until a visiting or sick relative came to stay—a frequent occurrence. Then, even if I were studying for finals, or going through a period when I desperately needed a place of retreat, I was expected to share. I rarely complained. I liked being thought of as the "good daughter, the dependable one." That was part of my survival kit.

When I was living in my tenement in New York, I never considered it home. It was makeshift, temporary, furnished with leftover lumber and material from old stage sets. It had an uninterrupted view of the dirty brick walls and grimy windows of a factory that made draperies. During the summer, with the windows open, I could depend on playing out my day's activities to the accompaniment of the nerve-shattering clackety-clack of fifty sewing machines. It was a place one craved to get away from.

On a different level, that's how I viewed my apartment throughout my married years. It was never quite mine. I felt uncomfortable spending large sums on things I liked. What did I like, anyway? With the exception of a few pieces, I bought furniture I figured my husband would like, or because it was serviceable for children, or because it was a bargain. And I rarely took chances: colors were conservative; nothing was daring enough to cause a controversy. The profusion of books and records, and the endless procession of animals, had come into the house over my protests.

In retrospect, I see that my protests lacked conviction. For one thing, I expected my feelings to be disregarded; hadn't they always been in the past? Secondly, I was getting some paltry status from the books and records and animals. As much as I detested the clutter, I liked hearing people comment on the impressiveness of our bookshelves: we were intellectuals; we had a mini lending library; it gave me an opportunity to recommend reading material, to advise, to be an authority.

The animals, which included mice, hamsters, gerbils, snakes, toads, frogs, turtles, iguanas, chameleons, fish, guinea pigs—and I could go on and on—elicited remarks such as: "Wow! You're not afraid to hold snakes? You're fantastic!" Or: "I don't know any other mother who would be willing to keep mealworms in her refrigerator and earthworms in her closet" (translation: "I don't know any other mother who would be such a patsy"). My son said I was "the greatest"—at least when it came to animals—and everyone was terribly complimentary about my superior knowledge of reptiles and rodents: "Call Greta if you have any animal questions. She knows everything."

I spent seventeen years in conflict: on the surface I played the super-understanding mother-and-wife role, always trying to go along with the demands and whims of husband and child; underneath I raged at the mess and dreamed of a home over which I'd have some control. Ironically, despite my fervent dream, even after my husband had left the house I hesitated about making many changes. I'd get to it in the future, I told myself, when I had money, when I could do things up just right.

The future, however, was beginning to seem too far off. As my needs came pushing to the surface, I recognized that I couldn't wait for perfection—just another way of postponing taking charge? I wanted satisfaction in the present. Most of all, I wanted a prettier study. Right now it was so heavy and dark: the battleship-gray desk lamp; the window blinds that cut off light; the black chair (the rush seat was okay); and especially the dark blue hi-riser cover. As I typed away one summer afternoon in 1976, I felt my eyes continually drawn to the offending fabric across the room. I hated the color with a passion. It had been chosen for a man's office; it had nothing to do with me. I found that I couldn't work as long as that cover remained in the room. There was no remedy but to remove it. I immediately pulled it off, bundled it into a package for the good old thrift shop, and went back to work.

Only now I was faced with two bare mattresses and the black frame of the hi-riser. How could I concentrate when confronted with such ugliness? With a sigh, I put aside my work, grabbed some charge cards, and made my way downtown to Macy's and Gimbels. Just let me find something light-looking, something I can afford, I kept repeating as the subway bore me toward 34th Street. Someone must have heard my wish because I found what I was looking for very quickly: a brown-and-white polka-dot, cotton-quilted cover with two bolster covers—price: twenty-five dollars. Next I picked up four throw pillows patterned in shades of yellow, green, orange, brown, and white—and they were on sale! As soon as I put the cover and the pillows on the hi-riser, I could see the beginnings of a different room.

For the rest of the day I was a whirlwind of activity: the shades were taken down, and hanging green plants were put in their place; I bought a can of bright yellow paint and went to work on my desk lamp and the black frame of my desk chair; next I filled ceramic pots with dried yellow and white flowers and placed them around the room; I bought a floor plant for $8—an amount that seemed enormous at the time—and put it near my desk by the window and then surrounded it with three smaller plants. I put two other small plants on one of my recently emptied bookshelves. Last of all, I tossed out the dark blue container that held my pencils and the dark brown wooden rack in which I filed letters. In their places, I substituted a yellow cup and a large, flowered ceramic pot.

At first everything seemed too much, too bright. The desk lamp suddenly loomed like a yellow beacon. Had I gone too far with my desire to get away from drabness? Would I have to redo the whole thing?

Take it easy, advised my rational self. Allow time to get accustomed to the new colors. It will take a while to get used to your individuality; it's very new for you.

And so I just sat for about a half hour and let the feel of the room become familiar. By then I could see that it wasn't too much at all. It was wonderful. Although the windows faced north, everything was sunny and bright. Maybe it wasn't a decorator's dream, but it was exactly the way I wanted it. As my eyes wandered around the room, surveying the results of my very modest efforts, I couldn't help getting all choked up and teary. I felt a fool, but dammit! this was a major event in my life. Finally, at the age of forty-eight, I had a room of my own.

A few months later, another dream was fulfilled; I had a stereo of my own. That came about through an incident that occurred at a party I gave in December of 1976. The party was a departure from any party I'd given in the past. It did not feature lots of food, and it was not composed of a selected few who were guaranteed to get along famously with one another. I invited forty-five people to come to my

house on a Saturday evening between the hours of six and
eight. I served wine, raw vegetables with a dip, and cheese.
Before deciding on such a party, I had gone through my
usual worrying routine. Would there be enough food? (During my married days I had considered a huge spread essential.) Would people be satisfied with my inexpensive wine?
What about the wine mavens or the beer drinkers or the
scotch addicts? Would everyone show up for a party given
by a woman alone? Would they put in a token appearance
and then leave early? For once, the only thing I didn't worry
about was money. This kind of an evening I could afford.

It turned out to be the most enjoyable party I'd ever
given. Almost everyone came, and a great many friends
stayed on until ten o'clock. Not one person complained of
a lack of food or of the absence of hard liquor. In addition,
I had great fun. Because I didn't have to serve or cook or
mix drinks, I had plenty of time to visit with my guests.

One of the women guests, who had never been to my
house before, brought me a record featuring Luciano Pavarotti and Mirella Freni singing arias from *Madame Butterfly*.
She looked stricken when she discovered that I had nothing
to play it on. "I'll take it back," she had volunteered. "I'll
get you something else."

"No. Don't do that," I had responded without thinking.
"Your timing is perfect. I'm buying a stereo tomorrow." A
minute later I realized what I had said and almost fainted.
But I had made the commitment, and I was not going to
go back on it. Besides, I was dying to hear all my records
that had sat unplayed for three years. Clearly it was time!

The next day I clipped an ad for hi-fi equipment that was
on sale for $350. I had wanted something better, but this
was the most I could afford. I checked my bank balance
to assure myself that my extravagance wouldn't put me out
on the street and went nervously off to make my purchase.

"If you could pay a little bit more," the very nice salesman said, "I could give you a really fine receiver."

"Gee, I don't know," I had answered weakly. "I'm a wreck spending this much."

He had nodded sympathetically and had gone off to get the components. He returned, bearing several large boxes and smiling broadly.

"I have good news," he announced jubilantly. "We're out of the advertised receiver so I have to give you one of equal quality or better." He winked at me. "I'm giving you the one that's better. You're going to love it." He seemed so genuinely happy for me that I forgot my fear of poverty and wrote out the check with barely a quiver of the hand.

It was one of those days when everything goes right: When I left the store, although it was rush hour, I found an empty cab immediately; the cab driver was intelligent and charming; my friends from upstairs, who three years ago had helped me rearrange my furniture, were available to help me hook up the equipment.

That night I played a few of my records. It was so exciting. It was like rediscovering old friends. And was I imagining things or was it true that they sounded better than they had ever sounded on my husband's hi-fi? I was sure they did. At one point, as I curled up on the couch to hear the new *Madame Butterfly* record, I thought with amazement: I'm having such fun! Even if there were a "special someone" with me, I don't think I'd enjoy myself one bit more. In fact, it might even be a little unpleasant: maybe we'd disagree over what records to play; or perhaps he'd want the volume up and I'd want it down. Oh, I'm so glad I'm alone. It's a perfect evening.

The following night was New Year's Eve and my forty-ninth birthday. For the first time in twenty years I was spending it solo—just me and my stereo. I put on Glenn Gould playing Mozart sonatas, pulled a book from the bookshelves, and poured myself a glass of good red wine.

Well, I mused, as I settled into the big chair and put my

feet up on the hassock, it's not too bad to celebrate this way. I kind of like it. I do get a little squirmy wondering if other people will pity me because no one has asked me out for New Year's Eve. But the truth is, I can't think of a single person—man or woman—I'd like to share this evening with. That last thought made me sad. I so wanted to feel close to someone.

But right now you don't, my rational self commented bluntly. No sense fretting about it.

Quite right, I acknowledged, very happy to be relieved of the burden of sadness. I smiled contentedly and opened my book to Chapter One. A couple of hours later, just before midnight, I put down my book, flipped the knob on my receiver from phono to tuner, refilled my empty wine glass, and waited. Soon a male voice announced: "It's twelve o'clock, everybody. Happy New Year! Happy 1977!" And then the familiar strains of "Auld Lang Syne" came pouring out of my two new speakers.

I raised my glass in a toast. "Happy birthday, Greta, old girl," I said a trifle drunkenly. "Happy New Year." I wanted to add something profound—a reflection or a prophecy—but I couldn't think of anything appropriate. So, instead, I drained my glass, turned off the tuner, threw chaste kisses to to the tuner, turntable, and both speakers and, feeling pleasantly light-headed, went to bed.

Chapter IX

Screw the whole damn thing! Three callbacks for a
play and it will probably go to someone else. Who
needs it? If I'm going to lose in this business, why
the hell can't I get out? Why the hell can't I quit?
It's just stupid to eat my heart out. Right now I'm
on this goddamn Fire Island-to-New York train with
a bunch of goddamn teen-agers and I've never felt
so rotten. I don't want to ride on a train with teen-
agers. I want to work with the grownups. I've got to
get into something else. I've got to quit playing a
losing game.
—From my journal, July 16, 1965

I began 1977 with optimism. Especially in the area of
work. I had finished my second book for young people and
was embarked on a third; I had a couple of magazine assignments; I was about to do my first workshop for women
alone; I had started collaborating with a crafts expert on
an adult book on how to make objects out of scrap—
lamps out of bottles, tabletops out of beach glass, toys
out of milk containers and egg cartons. I was busy and
productive and felt that, at last, I was well on my way to
conquering the no-money anxieties. And then March produced a lull, and I was back in my rocking chair railing at
myself for my stupid sense of false security. How could I
be such a fool as to let things get out of hand once again?
Would I ever learn to provide for the difficult times? What
was I to do? I felt so alone, so without resources.
"What a failure I am!" I cried aloud. "And when I try to

come up with a great solution, all I can think of is temporary typing. My God! Is that all I'm good for?"

Coincidentally, I had recently completed an article on temporary employment. I had interviewed a dozen intelligent, capable women between the ages of twenty and seventy who chose to work on a temporary basis, rather than lock themselves into full-time jobs. They had acknowledged there were drawbacks, but they liked the freedom and the variety. None had felt demeaned by the work. Moreover, they had all commented that it was gratifying to know that whenever they wanted a few days' work they needed only to pick up the phone. I had concluded the piece by pointing out that one of the most valuable aspects of temporary employment is that it provides ". . . a way to make money now when you need money now."

Sitting in my rocking chair, I recalled those words. I had to admit that at this moment they certainly applied to me. I needed money *now*! So what was I waiting for?

The following morning I put on my downtown clothes and, with a depressing sense of déjà vu, presented myself at the office of Adult Temps. Two hours later, after a typing test and an interview, I went home with the knowledge that on the morrow I would start a three-day stint at Park Printing Inc.

Park Printing was all my nightmares come true. The office resembled a cage: dirty, gray-green walls; dirty, gray-green metal partitions between offices; gray-green filing cabinets; dirt-filmed windows that let in no ray of sun. A middle-aged woman, with a gray-green complexion, gave me my instructions. I was to type up bills that were to be sent to customers. She led me to a battered desk whose top was adorned with a manual typewriter, piles of paper, and a stale-smelling, encrusted ashtray. I wanted to weep.

Next, the woman laid out the handwritten bills I was to copy. I glanced at one which appeared to be written in a foreign language.

"Excuse me," I said to the woman, struggling to keep the despair out of my voice, "I'm not sure I can make out all the words. Could you tell me what they mean?"

"Oh!" she responded with exasperation. "Don't you know our jargón? I particularly asked for someone who knew printing jargón."

"I'm afraid I don't," I answered, too miserable even to smile at her unusual pronunciation. "But," I almost pleaded, "you could call Adult Temps and they'll send you someone else." Escape! I was going to be able to get out of there!

"No, that's all right," the woman replied with evident concern for me. "You don't have to lose a day of work. You can spend the time adding up some figures for us. But," she had apologized, "I can't keep you on for the next two days. I'll need somebody who's familiar with our jargón."

Little did the woman know that not only wasn't I familiar with the "jargón," I was a dud at figures—even with an adding machine. I'm sure I made such a muddle of their arithmetic that some poor soul had to spend several days unraveling my mistakes. It was a hideous day; my head throbbed from the overhead fluorescents and the unending rows of figures that paraded before my eyes. The eight hours stretched out like eighteen. At five o'clock I dashed out of that office into the car-and-bus-filled streets and took my first deep breath of the day. Never had New York air smelled so sweet. It took me the forty-block walk home to begin to feel normal again.

From then on it could only get better, and it did. I typed briefs at a law firm and worked on the final draft of the year-end report at a bank. The bank executives were so pleased with my effort that they gave me an extra hour's pay. I walked home on air.

I was discovering that, far from demeaning me, the typing jobs were giving me a sense of well-being. I was bringing in extra money (I always brought my lunch and worked through the lunch hour. That way I'd get paid for eight hours instead of seven); my work was always complimented; I was no longer anxious about paying bills. I also found that I wasn't in the least embarrassed to tell people what I was doing. On the contrary, I was proud of myself. There were, however, those who viewed my endeavors with pity.

"You're doing temporary typing?" my literary agent friend Melanie exclaimed. "Oh, dear! You shouldn't have to stoop to that."

"I don't mind," I assured her. "It's honest work and I'm doing it well. Besides, it's helping me pay my bills."

She looked at me thoughtfully, all traces of pity gone from her face. "Listen," she said. "Maybe you'd like to type some of my authors' manuscripts. You could do it at home and you'd make more money."

Would I? You bet I would! I could start immediately.

And so I bid farewell to Adult Temps and began typing manuscripts. It was fascinating. By working on other writers' novels and non-fiction projects, I could see how they were constructed. I began to understand why something worked and why it didn't. It also helped me to look at other writers more realistically; it was obvious they weren't all paragons of excellence. They had problems similar to mine: some of their sentences were awkward, some repetitious; some of their ideas weren't clearly stated. I was aware that a few of the manuscripts I was typing as final drafts would no doubt have to go through at least one more draft before they would be ready for publication.

When I started typing manuscripts, I charged a dollar a page. After a few weeks, I recognized that I was pretty good and upped my rate to a dollar and a quarter. A month later, I felt confident enough to charge a dollar fifty. Not exactly the success story of the year, but it was more evidence for me that I could do things well.

At the end of April, I was offered thirteen fifteen-minute

radio shows to write. The shows featured a host and hostess who announced records, then played them, then commented on them. I was to write the cliché-ridden dialogue: "Hey! Here's an oldie that will set your hands a-clapping." Or: "Gee, Fred. Doesn't that one take you back to the good old days?" Writing that stuff nearly drove me out of my mind, but I couldn't afford to turn the job down. Therefore, when I wasn't working on my own projects, I'd spend half the time typing manuscripts and the other half wracking my brain to come up with the requisite idiot patter for the radio spots.

One reason why money was so scarce was because my collaborator on the crafts book was holding up its completion. That meant that the final payment of our advance was also being held up. As 1977 progressed, it began to look as though it might be held up indefinitely.

The question I asked myself over and over again was what was I doing in this collaboration in the first place. My answer was that I didn't know, that I had gone into it as unthinkingly as I had gone into my various "love relationships."

I had been offered the project in the summer of 1976 and had turned it down; writing how-to books was not high on my list of priorities. When it was again offered to me in the fall—apparently no other writer was panting to do it—I was feeling my familiar money panic, and I said I'd consider it. Before making up my mind, however, I went up to Connecticut to meet Thorsten, the crafts expert who would be my collaborator.

Thorsten turned out to be a dour, opinionated, smug man in his fifties. He bored me to death with his droning on about the various objects that would be included in the book. During lunch, I widened my eyes to keep them from closing as Thorsten explained at wearying length how this book would make all other crafts books unnecessary.

When I returned to New York, I called my agent and with a notable lack of enthusiasm agreed to take on the project. "I'm just doing this to keep myself afloat financially," I emphasized.

Since Thorsten lived in Connecticut, our arrangement was that he would send me chapters filled with information, and I would rewrite them in my own inimitable, perky, how-to style. I would send the chapters back to Thorsten, who would make corrections and additions. I would then do a final draft. What I hadn't counted on was that Thorsten couldn't type. He wrote in longhand, with the palest of pencils, on pages and pages of lined, yellow, legal paper. Any other writer would have said, "Listen, Buster, get this typed before you send it to me. If you don't, you can get yourself another writer." Not I. By then I was convinced that I needed the project, that I was lucky to have it, that I shouldn't make waves or I might lose it. My feelings were all too similar to those I'd experienced with Stuart, Andrew, and Josh.

I spent long hours trying to decipher Thorsten's D-minus penmanship, and a fortune in long-distance calls during which I begged for clarification. In addition, I went over his copy with my own dark black pencil, deleting his peculiar jokes (I was discovering that sour Thorsten considered himself something of a humorist, and he was indignant that I was delegating his prose to the wastebasket). Our various difficulties notwithstanding, and despite the fact that Thorsten never considered a chapter quite perfect enough—if he'd had his way we would have spent a year revising Chapter One—the book progressed. I was even beginning to enjoy it and grudgingly admitted that it had the potential for being an interesting and helpful manual.

The big snag came when we got to the chapter on objects made from tin cans. For some inexplicable reason, Thorsten felt this was the key chapter to the entire book, and he was determined to treat it with the solemnity and scholarship it deserved. He sent me fifty smudged, incomprehensible pages, the subject of which can only be described as "the philosophy of tin cans." I went berserk.

"Thorsten," I yelled into the phone, "I don't know what the hell you're trying to say. Just tell me simply how to make objects from the cans."

But Thorsten was obdurate. He'd rewrite it, but he still wanted to express his philosophy. He just knew that this chapter would set the book apart from all others (you bet it would). That chapter went back and forth between us at least ten times, until one day, after I'd sent it off for yet more corrections and additions, it never came back to me. Puzzled, I called Thorsten and got his answering machine. He didn't return my call. He didn't return subsequent calls, either. Nor did he answer any of my letters. In fact, I never heard from him again.

My agent and the editor talked to him and were told that I didn't understand him, that he was having difficulties getting across the essence of this very important chapter, that he wasn't sure he'd be able to complete the book. Eventually he cut off all communication with them, as well.

Through the months of working on the book, I had complained bitterly about Thorsten to my therapist. Early on, when I had raged because of his slowness, his inability to let go of a chapter, she had observed that if I had evaluated him more carefully in the beginning I would have foreseen the problems, and I wouldn't be feeling so angry and helpless now. Then she had added:

"You think you're lucky that Thorsten has allowed you to do this book with him. In truth, he can't do the book without you—or without someone like you. It's time you became aware that you're making a sizable contribution. It's also time you began to think about what you're getting out of this project. Does it have value for you? Do you really want to work with Thorsten? If you do, what are the things you like? What don't you like? You make the decisions. Don't leave your fate in Thorsten's hands."

She was right on target. When I first went to meet Thorsten, I had felt needy for money; I hadn't wanted to think

too much about the negative aspects of the book. I was going
to plunge in and do my job and just assume everything
would turn out dandy. What a fool I'd been. When did life
ever work that way? And wasn't it true that when I didn't
think things through in the beginning they always had unhappy endings?

Taking my therapist's advice, I began to go over the advantages and disadvantages of working on this project. Yes,
Thorsten was a pain, but the book was getting interesting.
I really didn't want to abandon it. It was the kind of book
that could possibly make me some money over a long period
of time. That wasn't to be sneezed at. My decision, finally,
was to stick with it. But I would also take into account
Thorsten's problems and irrationalities, and I'd try not to get
involved with them. For example, his slowness: there was
no way I could change that. But I could change how I reacted to it. His snail's pace was making me wild because I
wanted to finish and get our money. If I found some other
source of income—e.g., temporary typing—I could alleviate
that anxiety.

When Thorsten disappeared, I ranted to my therapist that
nobody—not my agent, not the editor—was doing anything
to rectify the situation. She then suggested that perhaps
there was nothing that could be done, and maybe it was
time to put the project behind me and to go on to something
else.

"How can I just walk away from it?" I shouted. "I've completed two-thirds of the book. Is all that work to go for
nothing?"

"You've learned from the experience," was her calm reply.
"That's hardly nothing."

"But if I abandon the project, I'll have to give back the
money."

"Maybe it would be worth giving up the money just to
get away from something that is not giving you very much
satisfaction." Again she repeated that I should make the

decisions, rather than let Thorsten or my agent or the editor make them for me.

In the end, the decision was made for me. Since Thorsten had gone into hiding, and since the editor didn't want to go through the legal hassle of bringing in a new crafts expert, there was no alternative but to put the project behind me. At least I didn't have to give back the money. With a sigh of resignation, I placed the folder containing all those neatly typed pages into my file drawer. (I almost cried as I recalled how I had painfully transcribed Thorsten's scribbles.) Chalk up one lousy experience. Next time I'd follow my intuition right from the start.

Alas, the next time was almost a repetition of the first time. And there was a third time and a fourth time. The lessons I had learned about personal relationships were all but forgotten when it came to working relationships. It almost seemed that having abandoned the quest for the perfect lover, I was hell-bent on finding the perfect collaborator. Even though I had completed three young-adult books, countless articles, foundation reports, cassettes, and publicity pieces, I still felt unequal to tackling an adult book all by myself. I was getting into the big leagues, and I was fearful of going it alone. I wanted a perfect partner to lean on: We'd be like Rodgers and Hammerstein; Comden and Green. I took on projects I had no heart for, with people with whom I had little rapport, just so I wouldn't have to work by myself. All of them ended in disappointment.

My rational self constantly pointed to the fact that in each collaboration I was doing most of the work. They're collaborations in name only, I told myself. You're kidding yourself if you think you're part of a team. You're on your own, and you don't even know it.

But I wasn't ready to give up the search. In the spring of 1977, it occurred to me that a book about psychotherapy, as practiced by my therapist, would be terrific. Her techniques and concepts had helped me make so many changes. Why not present them to the world so that others could make similar changes? Wouldn't it be great if my therapist and I could collaborate? When I approached her with the proposal, she explained that our therapist-client relationship negated any other relationship. "But you don't need me," she had added. "You can do the book alone."

I patiently explained the impossibility of her suggestion. "I'm not an expert in the field like you are," I told her. "I don't have the proper credentials for such a book."

"You could write about your own psychotherapy," she had pointed out. "You don't need credentials for that. No one is more of an expert on your life than you are."

She was making me *very* nervous. I'd come to her with visions of a partnership, and she was telling me to work alone. I had wanted to use her expertise, and she was claiming I was an expert. She was pushing me out of the nest, and I didn't like it.

And yet I was intrigued. I couldn't get the idea out of my mind. Even as I took on a new collaboration, I was mulling over her suggestion. It was tantalizing. As much as it frightened me, I wanted to give it a try. I wrote up a proposal describing the therapeutic process at length. My book, I explained, would show how that process had worked for me. I used a lot of technical words—"jargón," as the woman at Park Printing would say. I didn't want to leave any doubt that I was knowledgeable about psychology.

An editor friend read my proposal and gave the following opinion: the idea was good, but she wasn't crazy about all the technical discussion. Why didn't I just talk about myself in simple terms? How about showing my struggle, my feelings, my fears, my faults, my triumphs? I didn't have to sound like a Ph.D. in psychology to make my points.

I was getting nervous all over again. I had started off wanting to write a nice scholarly book in collaboration with an amiable, intelligent woman. When that hadn't worked out, despite my trepidation I had been willing to try the project alone. Now I was being told *that* wasn't enough. Why did each new recommendation push me further and further away from my moorings? Not only should I stand alone, but I was being asked to strip away all my defenses. Was there no end to it?

Okay! I'd do it. I'd gone this far, why not take the next step? I wrote a very simple proposal with two short chapters—very personal, very honest, and very painful to write. I also enclosed information about my workshop to indicate that my experiences had benefited other women. My friend loved it. My agent liked it. To my astonishment, it sold—with the proviso that I would include workshop chapters.

Good grief! I thought. What have I done? Now I have to write the whole book. I was so depressed by the vision of the enormous task ahead of me that I didn't even want to talk about my good fortune. Maybe if I didn't say anything, it would go away.

In September 1978, when my current collaborative venture was in the process of disintegration, I pulled myself together and began work on my solo venture. It was slow starting. I wanted to make this book important, vital. I felt I must find just the right words. I'd pace the study, type a little, pace some more, go out for a walk, come back, hit the typewriter again. I wrote, rewrote, tore up countless pieces of papers, until one day things started to move; yes, I could feel the energy building. It looked as if I'd be able to do it. After I'd completed three chapters, I read them over. Hey! They were pretty good! I almost broke my arm patting myself on the back. Very informative, I told myself. The writing's not bad, either. And soon paper was going in and out of my typewriter at a very brisk clip. By February, I had turned out eight chapters. I read them all through and pronounced them "not bad at all." I sent them off to my editor and waited impatiently for her praise.

She called me a week later, not with words of enthusiasm,

but to ask me to come in and go over the chapters with her.

"How do they seem to you?" I inquired, still waiting for her little chirps of delight over my super-terrific prose.

Her answer was hardly one to make the heart leap with joy. "They're okay." Her tone was cautious. "But they need work. Come on in tomorrow and we'll go over them."

When tomorrow came, it was a downer. My beautifully typed manuscript was full of editorial markings. Over and over again my editor had commented in the margins: "Too preachy"; "You sound like a schoolteacher here"; "Don't use clichéd psychological terminology"; "Needs more of a personal touch."

I was aghast. It was as though I were reading the manuscript for the first time. Her comments were all absolutely correct. My writing sounded so stilted. Why hadn't I noticed that at home? It wasn't at all my usual style. It could have been written by someone else. What had possessed me to write that way?

For six hours, as we went through the chapters, I continued to shake my head in disbelief. It wasn't until we had turned the last page that I felt that famous light bulb go on over my head.

"I've got it!" I exclaimed, just as they do in the comics. "I see what I've done. I've tried to write in my therapist's voice. Even though I wasn't collaborating with her, I was still trying to bring her into the picture; that way I wouldn't have to be completely alone. Isn't that wild?"

"It really is," my editor replied, her eyes wide. "Is that how your therapist sounds?"

"No. Not really. She's not preachy or schoolteacherish at all, and she rarely uses big psychological words. She's a very down-to-earth person. But I see now that I've lifted some of her expressions, and I've put them into long, pedantic speeches. I was trying to sound like an 'authority figure' so I'd be taken seriously. It's all wrong. It's not me. I've been afraid to use my own voice." Embarrassed, I looked at my editor: "You must have been horrified when you read all this. You must have wondered what you'd bought."

"No, I wasn't horrified at all," she said. "I knew something was wrong, but I also knew you could fix it." Her words warmed my heart.

I left the publisher's office armed with the marked-up manuscript. It felt very heavy. I would have to start over again. This time around, there would be no reaching for another identity, no hiding behind a flow of technical phrases. For better or worse, I would have to be me: my own expressions, my own feelings. And hadn't I done just that in my first two chapters? Why had I stopped? I must have gotten frightened being myself; it was so new for me. Whew! Thank goodness for second chances.

The next day I sat down to my typewriter, inserted a piece of paper, typed out the chapter heading, and stopped. I sat for awhile staring at the paper, hearing the words begin to take shape in my head. I began to type. The words formed on the paper, all of them in my own voice.

Chapter X

I've been thinking about my capabilities and liabilities, and I've decided to write them down.
Capabilities: 1. Good voice for acting and singing.
2. Good-looking.
3. Fairly good actress.
4. Possibly good writer.
5. Enjoy children.
Liabilities: 1. Not fully trained voice.
2. Not a good salesperson for my talents.
3. Giver-upper: Not ready to commit myself to anything long-term.
One thing I see now is that I'll be able to make a go of being a mother because I'm stuck doing it. Can't pull out at any whim. In a funny way, I'm not 100 percent committed to that, either. But I seem to be getting better.
—From my journal, February 25, 1966

If 1977 was a year of confronting the reality of my various collaborations, it was also a period of coping with the growing complexity of my son. He was fifteen, a young man with long hair, a deep voice, and a sprinkling of pimples and patches of beard on his once pure complexion. He had a life of his own, new friends, secrets that were not shared with mother. I'd hear him laughing and whispering with his buddies behind the closed door of his room. He and his friends played music I wasn't familiar with. They strummed guitars, beat on his newly purchased drum set, and exchanged confidences. If someone came out, the door was quickly shut so that the adult in the house—me—would not be privy to all the "fascinating" goings-on.

I saw myself as an outsider, a pariah. None of those kids wanted to chat with me, to benefit from my wisdom, to ask about my activities. Aside from a quick "Hi" as they made their way down the hall to my son's room, I was virtually ignored.

When my son and I were alone, our relationship was abrasive, to say the least. He was constantly at me for increased privileges, money, attention. He put me down every other minute and snapped at me if I made the smallest demand. I sometimes felt as though he wanted to pick and pick at me until I died. There were times, as he harangued me in the kitchen while I chopped vegetables, that the urge to sink my chopping knife into his gizzards was overwhelming.

Once, when I was feeling particularly oppressed by this person I was living with (never in my wildest dreams had I envisioned spending my middle years alone with a teen-aged boy), I had an image of my son choking me and dragging me underwater. I was startled to recall that something very similar had actually occurred at Lake Arrowhead when I was ten. I had been playing around in the shallow part of the lake when I hit a drop-off and suddenly found myself in water over my head. I wasn't much of a swimmer in those days but I could dog-paddle, and I immediately started my puppy-like motions to get myself back into the shallow area.

My mother, who was sitting on the beach, mistook my dog-paddling for flailing-about-to-keep-from-drowning movements and, forgetting that she couldn't swim at all, dashed into the water to save me. When she hit the drop-off, my mother panicked. She screamed for help and grabbed me around the throat. "Save me," she cried, her fingers tightening on my neck. Frantically, I struggled to get free, but she hung on as though I were a life raft. Seconds later, we were underwater. Luckily, my father heard the screams. He dashed into the water, grabbed my mother, and carried her, dripping and sobbing, from the lake. I was left to rub my neck and to try and steady my shaking legs, until a kindly lifeguard took pity on me and helped me ashore.

Wasn't that the story of my life? I thought ruefully. Even when my mother wanted to save me, she ended up practically killing me. Not only that, she got the sympathy, while I was scolded for going out over my head. And wasn't my son a chip off the old block? Like my mother, he was out to get me at every turn.

My therapist remarked, during one of our sessions, that my son demanded my attention by being unpleasant and abusive because he didn't feel I was very interested in him. "I don't mean he should be allowed to get away with that kind of behavior," she added. "You've got to call him on it. On the other hand, it's important you see that by not paying attention to him you play a part in all this."

"How can you say I'm not interested in him, that I don't pay attention to him?" I asked irritably. "I'm constantly listening to his problems and his complaints. A day doesn't go by that I'm not listening. He's killing me with his complaints and his needs."

"You don't *really* listen," she replied. "Very often you don't listen here. You're very quick to defend yourself, to argue, to dismiss anything you don't immediately agree with. You often try to come up with quick answers. You don't mull over what's been said, you don't take the time to evaluate. You grew up with parents who either put you down or spouted irrationalities, and you're accustomed to tuning most people out. Not everyone, however, is as irrational as your parents were. Not everyone is so ready to put you down."

I thought a lot about her words. Could she possibly be right? I watched myself with people, especially with my son. Was I truly not paying attention, not evaluating, not thinking about the other person? It was hard for me to accept such a picture of myself. I had always believed that I was a good listener, someone who had a knack for drawing people out. But maybe I just went through the motions; maybe I wasn't actually hearing what was being said.

In May I gave another party. It was much like the one I'd given in December, except that this time I included more food. I pulled down my vegetarian cookbook and had a grand old time concocting mushroom and bean patés, spiced cheeses, guacamole, stuffed grape leaves, and an assortment of dips for vegetables and crackers. In the morning of the day of the party, I told my son to shower and tidy up the bathroom before the guests came at six. He responded quite pleasantly that he would. That was unusual. As a rule, he gave me an argument. Maybe, for a change, he'd come through for me. But I wouldn't count on it.

By three o'clock, my son still hadn't showered. Wouldn't you know it! He was going to give me a hard time, after all. I decided not to say anything just yet; I'd wait another hour. At four, when he still hadn't showered, I reminded him—very nicely, I thought—that I wanted the bathroom empty and clean before the guests arrived. He became furious. He would shower when he damn well felt like it, he told me nastily. He didn't care whether the guests were here or not. He couldn't care less about my stupid party. He couldn't care less if the bathroom was clean or dirty. I started to shake with rage. Only a short time before the party and we were going into one of our terrible scenes. I couldn't bear it. I was not going to let it happen. I grabbed my purse and rushed from the house to do some last-minute shopping.

I was in the depths. All the way to the market, I repeatedly asked myself what had happened. The day had started out so

peacefully; why had it turned into a disaster? What was my
part in all of it? I felt I was blameless. All I'd done was make
a simple request, and all hell had broken loose.

My rational self argued that it hadn't been such a simple
request.

What was so complicated? I just said I wanted him out of
the bathroom before the guests came.

Ah! But you said it twice.

So what! Don't I have a right to make a request twice?
Is that a crime? Is it so awful to . . . ?

But he told you in the morning he would do what you
asked, cut in my rational self. Obviously, you didn't hear him.

I heard him.

You may have heard him, but you didn't take him seriously. Right from the start, you were sure he'd let you down.
That's why you kept checking on him, worrying about
whether or not he'd do it. You couldn't let him alone to
handle your request in his own way and in his own time.
No. You had to needle him. That's not treating him with
respect.

So that's what the therapist had meant by not listening.
It wasn't that I didn't hear the words, it was just that I
didn't take the words seriously. Of course, there were other
times when I took the words too seriously: when my son
talked nonsense, I often treated his sentences like pure gold.
I wasn't accustomed to making distinctions. So I wasn't
blameless, after all.

When I returned home, I knocked on my son's door.

"Yeah?" He still sounded angry. "Whaddya want?"

"I want to apologize."

He opened the door. His face was tight, suspicious.

"I realize there was no reason for my having repeated my
request to you. I was showing a lack of trust in you." I
watched his features begin to soften. "You told me you'd do
what I asked, and that should have been enough for me.

I'm very sorry that I didn't leave you alone. I'll try to be more trusting in the future."

"Yeah. I was going to do everything before the people came," he mumbled, not looking at me. "Yeah. Well, thanks for apologizing. I gotta shower now." Then he added: "I'm glad we're not fighting anymore. I didn't want to fight when you were giving a party." He quickly closed the door.

I stared at the door with my mouth open. I'd done it! I had thought about what had happened, and I'd come up with a way to deal with it. I had listened. I had paid attention. And I had learned something about myself. My son had looked so relieved. His outburst had probably frightened and puzzled him as much as it had me—why had I always assumed he enjoyed our fights? He had wanted the antagonism to end but hadn't known what to do. He seemed grateful that I had found the solution. A few minutes later, it struck me: this was the first time I had ever apologized to him.

I'd be thrilled to report that from that day on I was always respectful and understanding in my dealings with my son. But I can't. There were other equally disturbing interactions, although as time went on they became fewer and fewer. One particularly painful incident occurred when I smelled marijuana coming from his bedroom. I burst into the room and caught two of his friends sharing a joint. I was indignant. How dare they smoke in my house? Without so much as a by-your-leave, I launched into my anti-marijuana lecture, and my son erupted. He screamed at me, he swore at me, he wanted to kill me. His friends looked on nervously.

And once again I had to acknowledge that I had caused the eruption. I had demeaned my son: I had gone into his room without knocking; I hadn't given the situation a moment's thought; I certainly hadn't evaluated what was going on—was it really *so awful*? Were they bothering me? If I had strong feelings, why couldn't I have waited and talked to my son privately, instead of embarrassing him in front of his friends? I had wanted to be heard, and nothing

was going to stop me. Like an old warhorse, I had invaded
the room and gone into my act. I was the star, they were the
supporting players. There was no corner of my son's life that
was safe from my intrusion. No wonder he had risen up in
anger. It was another time when I felt an apology was definitely in order.

Other smaller incidents began to come to my attention.
One evening my son came into the living room to tell me
about a book he was reading. He was very excited about it,
wanted to share it with me. And what did I do? Instead of
listening carefully to him, allowing him to bring something
to me, I became involved in my own thoughts: I'm so
pleased he's reading rather than watching television; if he's
enjoying that book, I bet he'd love *The Catcher in the Rye*. I
think I have a copy somewhere. My eyes began to scan the
bookshelves. When my son paused for a breath, I jumped
up and went toward the bookshelves. "I have a book you'll
just love," I said. "I'll find it for you."

"That's okay. I haven't finished this one yet." He watched
me search the shelves. "I think I'll go back and read."

When I turned around, he had left the room.

My rational self was appalled: What a pain-in-the-ass
mother you are. Every time your son opens his mouth, you
have to get into the act. And then you complain that he
doesn't want to talk to you. Who wants to talk to someone
who doesn't listen? Let him pick his own books. All you
have to do is pay attention to what he's saying—*really* pay
attention.

I was trying, but it was hard.

It was also hard coming to terms with my teen-aged son's
need for increasing freedom. We were constantly doing battle
over how late he should stay out on weekends. Initially, I
had established a curfew of midnight, but under pressure I
had upped it to 1 A.M. When he turned sixteen, I upped the
time to one-thirty. By then, however, my son wanted no
part of a curfew. He desperately wanted to determine his

own hours; I was equally desperate to keep some measure of control.

As long as we were in conflict, weekends were trying. The nights he'd observe the curfew were fine; I'd go to bed at midnight or 1 A.M. and fall asleep immediately. But I'd always awaken at one-thirty when the key turned in the lock of the front door—even with my bedroom door closed and the air-conditioner on, I'd hear that reassuring click and sigh with relief. He was home safe. I'd roll over and go back to sleep. On the nights when there was no sound of the key, I'd wake automatically at one-thirty. I'd switch on the light, check the clock, and become agitated. He was late! Where was he? I'd wait fifteen minutes, and, if he still hadn't come home, I'd start calling his friends. Did they know where he was? Someone always did. His friends treated me very patiently, as though I were an overly anxious mother they had to humor—which, in fact, I was—and I'd hang up feeling furious at my son for putting me through this humiliation. He, of course, was full of excuses: "The party ran late, and I didn't want to call and wake you"; "The house didn't have a phone" (has anyone ever heard of a ten-room Park Avenue apartment that didn't have a phone?); "There were no clocks in the apartment"; "I had to wait an hour for a bus"; "The bus broke down coming across the park."

As time went on, coming home past the curfew became the rule, rather than the exception. I couldn't stand it anymore: I was tired of the constant involvement in my son's affairs; I was cranky from loss of sleep; I was not going to debase myself one more time by those rounds of calls to his friends. Something had to change.

My ideal choice would have been to transform my son into a loving, considerate young man who would obediently trot home at a set time every Friday and Saturday night. Or, if he were going to be late, he would consistently call me. But sixteen years of experience with him indicated that was highly unlikely. The change was going to have to come from me. So, feeling a failure as an enforcer of rules, I gave in and abolished the curfew. I told my son that he could make his own decisions about the hour to come home. He was old enough, responsible enough, and I was leaving it up to him. I didn't for a moment believe my words. Responsible? I was positive he was totally irresponsible, that given his freedom he would surely run wild. I was wrong. Once the curfew was lifted, he began to come home at very reasonable hours, sometimes even earlier than one-thirty—that would have been unthinkable during the curfew period. There were nights when he stayed out until three, and there were other nights when he came rolling in at five, but, for the most part, with no need to rebel, he began to be much more sensible about his social life.

And it worked wonders for me. A tremendous burden was lifted from my shoulders. I no longer felt compelled to make sure that nothing terrible happened to my son—did I really believe my worry would keep him safe? I didn't have to stay alert in case I was called on to handle an emergency. I could go to bed and sleep through the night. (Interestingly, I suddenly became deaf to the click of the key in the lock.) If there were an emergency, I'd hear soon enough. One more step in that long, letting-go process.

It was during one of those early weekend mornings that I inadvertently stumbled upon another puzzle piece from the past that helped me better understand the present. It occurred at 2 A.M. on Sunday. My son had just come home from a party, and the sound of his boots clumping down the hall had awakened me. I lay half asleep, listening to him go from his bedroom to the bathroom and back again. And then I was sitting bolt upright, my heart rocking so hard I thought it would burst out of my chest. My son was leaving the house! He was going away again! Yes! I could hear him opening the front door. Where was he off to at this late hour? I scrambled out of bed and ran down the hall. My son's door was closed. I went to the front door. It was locked, the chain was on. The back door was also locked and chained. He hadn't gone out at all, he had gone to bed. I had imagined the whole thing.

I went back to my room and got into bed. I was drenched in sweat, my head was throbbing, my heart still going like crazy. Why on earth had I become so terrified? Even if my son had gone out, what was so frightening about that? Did it have something to do with the past? As though on cue, a picture of myself in the small bed in the corner of my grandfather's room flashed before my eyes. Now I remembered. My parents had abandoned me to that room: a room of terrors, where shadows hung on the walls and ceilings and windows. My grandfather had lain in the big bed: a dark, ominous figure that thrashed about, growling and moaning. Every night he had tossed and turned while strange and eerie sounds had emanated from under the moving bedclothes. And every night I had lain in my bed, bathed in sweat and shaking, waiting, waiting. For what? For something awful to happen. For what? For that angry, dark figure to leap at my throat, to put his hands around my throat, and to . . . to what? To *squeeze and squeeze* until I couldn't breathe anymore.

Where had my parents been? Why hadn't they come to comfort me? Why hadn't they taken me out of that room of terrors? They had been far away in their own room. They had never heard the wild sounds of my grandfather's nightmares. Besides, *they* had put me in the room. *They* had sacrificed me. I couldn't go to them. I couldn't go to anyone. There was nobody to save me. I was alone in a room with death.

That last thought must have released some long-pent-up emotions, for I was suddenly weeping and sobbing uncontrollably. All the submerged pain was rising and gushing out onto the pillows and the sheets. It was a veritable flood of age-old anguish. I couldn't stop the flow, and I didn't want to. It felt so good. I was being purged of a dreadful weight that had held me down for much too long. I was becoming lighter than air.

When there were no more tears and I was peaceful and calm, I began to explore why I had reacted so intensely on this particular night. What was going on in my life that might have triggered the extreme fear? There were two things I could think of. One, I had been feeling increasingly estranged from my son lately. Two nights ago I had gone to bed early and had heard him in his room, laughing with three friends. I had been overcome with such a sense of isolation: he was part of a team, I was a solitary figure. I had been having similar feelings in connection with my work; my current collaboration was having its troubles, and I had just signed the contract for the book I would write alone. Once again I was all by myself, naked and vulnerable, just as I had been when I was a child sleeping in my grandfather's room. My parents had been a couple, they could protect each other. While I, the sacrificial lamb, lay waiting for death, they were snug in each other's arms in their own cozy room.

It all made sense; I could see the connection. My fear of my son taking on a life apart from me—a life I assumed to be carefree and warm, full of laughter and "togetherness" (Boy, was that a fantasy)—and my taking on a new venture alone had evoked some old, unresolved emotions. Suddenly I saw my son leaving me to be sacrificed to all the unseen evils. Only, I had overlooked one thing; I was no longer a child who could be sacrificed. I was the mother, the adult in the house. I was sleeping alone in my room out of choice. I was doing my book alone out of choice. My son's increased autonomy couldn't possibly condemn me to death. Indeed, my life was opening up so dramatically that I was more alive than ever. I could say good-bye to the trembling little girl in the small bed in the corner of the dark, shadowy room. I was in the big bed now, in the very center of my bright and airy room. I was in charge. There was nothing to fear.

Workshop V

Our last session. The women chat quietly for a few minutes, filling each other in on their past week's activities. There is an easiness among them as though they have been friends for a long time. As I listen to them I think, as I have thought with every workshop group, that when women get together and reveal their feelings, there's no such thing as a generation gap. I remember the first session of one workshop series. Two young women in their twenties were the last to arrive. They stood in the doorway surveying the room, and I could see the dismay on their faces. All the other women were over forty, and one woman was clearly in her sixties. They reluctantly took their seats, and the session began. For the first half hour neither young woman said much, but they were listening. And without their realizing it, they slowly became actively involved with what the others were saying. Soon they were revealing things about themselves, offering suggestions, asking advice. When the session was over, one of the women came up to me. "Boy!" she exclaimed. "That was terrific! And am I surprised! When my friend and I walked in here, I thought it would be a drag with all these older ladies. But we all have so much in common. I can't believe it!" Then she and her friend went off with the others to the coffee shop.

Laura's voice interrupts my thoughts. She is looking particularly exotic tonight in an Indian shirt and Indian necklace and earrings. She speaks across the circle to Julia: "I just heard of a new singles' place. It's for people our age, not for kids in their twenties. It's supposed to be really nice—not frantic and all that. It's the kind of place where they have lectures and discussions, and sometimes they all go to dinner together. Do you want to try it with me this weekend?"

Julia shakes her head no. "I'm through with that stuff for awhile. I've decided to take Greta's advice and concentrate on finding a better job. My son came over last night to help me work on my résumé."

Her statement animates the group. Ann, Connie, and I offer words of support, Susan and Laura express envious admiration, and Elaine asks what kind of job she's going to look for.

"I want to go into office management," Julia declares.

From Ann: "How come all of a sudden?"

"It's not all of a sudden. I've always hated bookkeeping, but I did it to help out my husband with his business. Then after he died I had to make money, so I kept on doing it. I didn't think I could do anything else. My son, Tod, has been after me for a long time to get into a job that requires management skills. He kept reminding me that, although I didn't realize it, I managed Phil's business." She smiles ruefully. "Looking back, I suppose I did. But for a long time I didn't want to listen to Tod because all his ideas involved so much effort. But I'm listening now." She looks at me. "I credit the workshop for that. You've shown me that I've got to start taking myself seriously, that it's stupid for me to do something almost every day of my life that I hate. So I'm going to change."

I notice that tonight Julia is a far cry from the subdued, defensive person of our first session. She even looks different. Instead of her usual beiges and browns, she is dressed in a purple skirt and a dusty-pink sweater. Her eyes are bright, and the pink of her sweater is reflected in the tint of her cheeks. How remarkable! I tell Julia that I'm so pleased she's been able to come to that decision. "It sounds like a positive step."

"I think so, too," is her reply. "Now that I'm looking at myself as a manager instead of a bookkeeper I'm excited. I've got ideas going on in my head. And you remember how in the first session I told you that nothing interested me? That's changed, too. The new approach to work has given me a new approach to other things."

Has it given her a new approach to her relationship with the man in her life? Ann wonders.

Julia maintains it has. "I don't have as much time to think about him as I did before. I don't know what's going to happen with us—maybe nothing." Julia shrugs. "But I'm not going to sit around worrying about it. I have other things to do, and that makes me a lot less angry at him." She nods emphatically. "Things are better."

The women are full of advice and suggestions for Julia's job search: Connie gives her the name of a very good agency that handles office management positions; Ann thinks she knows of a possible job opening—she'll check on it; Susan mentions that a friend of hers went to a career counselor who helped her construct a "fantastic" résumé. She'll get a copy for Julia on the chance that it might give her some ideas for making up her own.

Julia appears to be delighted with all the attention and help. She thanks everyone profusely for their interest.

When the last suggestion has been made, Elaine speaks. She confesses that she is jealous of Julia. "Julia is moving her life, and I'm standing still," Elaine observes sadly. "All week I've thought about what I should do, and I can't come up with any answers." She fixes me with a bewildered expression. "Do you think I need psychotherapy?"

"You don't *need* psychotherapy," I respond. "Nobody *needs* it. It's not a medicine you take for a sickness. You say you're upset because you're in a rut, and you don't know how to get yourself out and moving. A psychotherapist could be helpful to you if you're willing to do the required work."

Elaine continues to look puzzled. "What kind of work? If I do the work, what am I paying a therapist for?"

I point out that the therapist's job is to help her discover her hidden goals and to explain those goals to her so she can understand her behavior and begin to change it. But *she* would have to work. I can see by her expression that Elaine still doesn't grasp what I'm talking about. So I say: "You will have to dredge up the material to be analyzed in your sessions; you will have to think about what's discussed; then you will have to be willing to risk making changes. It's the process I outlined for you in the first session. Therefore, it's not that you *need* therapy, it's a question of whether or not you're interested in going that route."

We all look expectantly at Elaine. She seems close to tears, and her ringed fingers twist and untwist a tissue.

"I only know I'm miserable," Elaine confides, her voice husky. "I see Julia doing good things; Connie takes charge of her life; Ann is in charge of her life—she has all those friends; even Susan has made a little change by enrolling in school."

I wonder to myself if Laura is hurt because she's not included in the list.

Elaine goes on: "I'm doing nothing but waiting for something to happen." Tears fill her eyes and roll down her face, but she makes no move to wipe them away. She continues to twist and untwist the tissue which is now beginning to shred and fall to the floor. Elaine addresses me: "You've changed. You said psychotherapy helped you. Why couldn't it help me?"

Ann hands Elaine a fresh tissue, and I gently repeat that it can be helpful if she's willing to do the work. I then add that if she's interested I'd be very glad to give her some guidelines on how to choose a therapist.

After she has wiped her eyes and blown her nose, Elaine declares she is interested, that she would like some guidelines.

I begin by explaining that in choosing a therapist she has a right to do comparison shopping. In fact, I add, she absolutely should. She can get a referral from a friend who has made impressive changes in therapy, or she could get names from analytic institutes, feminist organizations, or even churches. Another possibility would be to write to a well-known therapist whose writings she admires and to ask him or her to suggest a couple of names—she might even want to find out if the famous person will take her on as a client.

"Famous people are expensive," Laura comments.

"They are," I agree. "It's just another suggestion."

Susan wonders if you have to pay for interviews, and I answer that you do—usually the therapist's hourly fee.

"That could end up costing a lot," she observes.

"It's true it could, but in the long run it's less costly than going into therapy with someone you don't know very much about. You could go to the person for months, at the rate of fifty dollars an hour, only to discover that you don't think too highly of him or her. Then you have to quit and go searching for someone else. That can be very painful, and you've wasted all that money. I think it's much sounder to spend one or two hundred dollars doing a little research. Not that that's a foolproof method," I hasten to add, "but it does give you some idea of what you're getting into."

I watch Elaine. She's no longer teary, and she's listening intently to everything that's being said. I tell her that even after she's started therapy, she's going to have to evaluate whether or not it's helping her.

Elaine interrupts. "Doesn't the therapist tell you how you're doing?"

"You're the only one who can know that," I respond. "You're the expert on you. So you have to figure out along the way if the whole process is making sense to you—it shouldn't be mysterious and strange with a lot of technical phrases. In the beginning, of course, your main concern will be to make yourself feel better."—Elaine nods vigorously—

"But after a few months you should be able to understand your behavior better, to handle anxiety to some degree, to feel a little freer about making choices."

"Isn't it funny," comments Susan, looking at Elaine with compassionate blue eyes, "even though I'm twenty-five years younger than Elaine, I understand exactly what she's going through."

"Me, too," reveals Laura.

I ask Susan what it is that she identifies with, and she answers that she shares Elaine's fear of doing things alone, of losing the "togetherness."

"Do you know," she confides, "that ever since I sent off that application to school I've felt so frightened? The other day I got the list of courses and their hours. In two months I'll be going to school two nights a week. That's two full nights, plus the other nights when I'll have to do homework, when I won't be able to be with my boyfriend. What's going to happen to the relationship?"

Susan's face is pale, and I can see that she is, indeed, very frightened. I tell her that I, too, have gone through similar bouts of anxiety, and, if it's any consolation, I've always emerged much stronger when I've worked through the anxiety and gone on to do what I set out to do. I add that if she wants to advance her work situation, it will involve taking risks; and one of the risks is the possibility of alienating her boyfriend. Only she can decide if it's a risk worth taking.

"I guess I want a guarantee that everything will work out okay." She looks pleadingly around the circle, apparently hoping that one of the women will give her the guarantee. The women can only smile sympathetically.

Ann says: "I think you should take the risk, Susan." Her round face is very warm and kind. "It's no good playing it safe. You can stick close to home, you can be compliant and sweet, and you can lose the guy anyhow. My husband left me when he felt like it, even though I always tried to please him. Make your own life. That way, if anything goes wrong you won't fall apart, as I did."

Susan is obviously touched by Ann's concern. She tells us she knows she'll hate herself if she doesn't stick with school. "I've started and I don't want to turn back," she states plaintively. "I guess I do want to take a chance." She grimaces. "I just hope I won't be sorry."

"I'd like to offer my help, Susan," Ann says. "If during the next few months you feel tempted to drop out, and you want to talk to someone before doing anything drastic, you can call me. And I'll be there to encourage you to stick with it."

Susan seems overwhelmed by Ann's offer. "Are you sure you wouldn't mind?"

"No, I wouldn't at all. I know what it's like to doubt your choices. And I know that it really helps to have someone out there to tell you you haven't done something crazy, that you're doing exactly the right thing. You're going to need that kind of reassurance, because your boyfriend will probably tell you just the opposite—especially on those nights when he wants to go out with you and you have to stay home and do homework."

Susan makes another face and confides that that's exactly what she's afraid of. She gazes gratefully at Ann and says she probably will take her up on the offer. I have the urge to caution Ann not to get manipulated into doing too much for Susan as everyone else seems to do, but I decide to let it go. Ann can handle things perfectly well on her own.

I remind myself that Laura, too, claimed an identification with Elaine. I ask her if she'd like to comment on her feelings.

Her face starts to become remote, and then I see her check herself. Apparently she's not going to withdraw, after all.

"Yeah," she says hesitantly, "I would. I think what gets me about Elaine is her not being able to come up with answers. Sometimes I feel paralyzed, and I think that's how

Elaine feels. It's like I'm trapped, like there's no way out, like I'll be in this same spot for the rest of my life." She turns to Elaine. "That's what you're talking about, isn't it?"

Elaine confirms that it is.

"What's even harder," Laura continues, "is that I'm always panicky. I keep wanting to think of a solution and I never can, and then the panic spills over into every part of my life. So I never can enjoy *anything*."

I mention to Laura that recently I had an experience where that kind of anxiety was permeating all my activities. "In my case," I say, "it was because I was getting irrationally terrified about money. I was thinking about money so much that I couldn't work, I couldn't fully enjoy social experiences. Finally, I hit on a very good plan. I determined to devote one hour every day to my money problems. I could use that time to explore how real my fears were, to think of ways for saving money, for earning money. It would be a period of full concentration on that one subject. I also determined that I would not think about the problem during any of the other hours of the day."

Laura looks skeptical and wonders if that kind of plan can work.

I assert that it can. "As soon as I focused on the problem during a specified period, I began to get a lot of ideas. In addition, it freed me to concentrate on my other activities."

Connie, who has been listening attentively, says she likes that idea. "I'm going to try it," she states. "In fact"—looking at me—"I've been meaning to tell you that I've been able to work through a few anxious moments by using some of the ideas you gave us during the second session. I think they're terrific. It's so much better than all the running-around stuff I used to do."

I tell Connie how glad I am that she's been able to use some of the things we've talked about. I suggest that if she, or Laura, or any of the other women want to use the allotted time each day—"And it doesn't have to be an hour," I say.

"It could be a half hour or two hours"—she should try not to force answers and solutions. I explain that it should be an ongoing process. If ideas are forthcoming during one session, fine. If not, she should go on to something else when the hour is up, with the knowledge that she'll be coming back to the problem the next day.

"I know what's bugging me," Laura suddenly exclaims. She faces the group, her mouth slightly open, her eyes wide with surprise. "Yeah!" she continues in a voice of wonder. "It's not that I think I'm going nowhere; that's not what's scaring me tonight. I'm scared because I went out and bought those damn dishes and didn't tell my mother."

The other women dissolve in laughter. Laura stares at them in bewilderment. "It's not funny," she says indignantly. "I don't know why you guys are laughing."

"We're not laughing at your problems," Ann says, trying to control her giggles. "We're laughing because you sounded so amazed and funny. We don't think *you're* funny, though. We think it's great that you finally did something without consulting dear old mother."

Laura permits herself a tentative smile. "Yeah! I did." She still sounds surprised. "And you know why I did? Because all of you made me feel like a jerk for not having bought them. So now I have the dishes and I'm too nervous to use them."

There's something very comedic about Laura's delivery, and it's with effort that the women refrain from breaking up again. I ask Laura what she thinks will happen as a result of her having bought the dishes.

"I don't know." Laura wrinkles her nose and ponders my question. Then she says: "I guess I'm afraid she'll yell at me and tell me how stupid I am. And maybe I am stupid. I mean, when I get married I may want entirely different dishes. So why have I wasted money now?"

I say: "Listen, Laura, since you're not planning to get married in the near future, that last statement is totally irrelevant. Secondly, even if you were getting married, there's no reason why you can't get one set of dishes now and another later on. Third, you've really got to start working on your relationship with your mother." Laura's eyes start to cloud over but I persist: "I can see you pulling back, and you've done that in every session when we've gotten close to something uncomfortable for you. But honestly, Laura, I feel it's imperative that you begin to come to terms with your mother. You've got to ask yourself why, at the age of thirty-eight, you're still so terrified of her; why, as a grown woman, you don't feel free to buy a set of dishes if she doesn't give permission. What are you getting out of all this? The years are running out, Laura," I continue passionately. "You're not a child anymore, you're an adult, and you're entitled to all the freedoms and responsibilities of an adult. It's time you realized that."

My words seem to have jarred Laura out of her withdrawal. She doesn't look particularly happy, however. She sits in silence, eyeing me suspiciously.

Connie speaks: "I have an idea, Laura. Why don't you invite all of us to a communal dinner, and we'll help you launch your dishes?"

Laura gazes warily around the circle. "Would you all want to come?"

The five women nod, and I see Laura start to relax. She agrees it's a good idea, and Connie presses her for a definite date. When the evening has been decided upon, the women discuss who will bring what foods. Soon everything is settled. Connie looks quite pleased to have come up with a helpful suggestion.

Laura makes no reference to my comments concerning her mother, and for the moment I don't bring it up again. I'd like to, but knowing Laura's difficulty with the subject I decide to wait for her to lead into it. That way she might be more receptive to pursuing it.

I hear Ann say: "By the way, Laura, are the dishes pretty?"

Laura's face lights up. "They're gorgeous," she answers. "I love them." Her expression changes to one of gloom. "I think that's why I'm so depressed. If they give me so much pleasure, something terrible will happen."

Now I figure I can say something. "You know, Laura," I begin carefully, "I'm very sympathetic with your feelings. Everytime I've treated myself to something wonderful, I've gone through agonies. I tell myself I've been too extravagant, I didn't *really* need whatever I bought, I'm being self-indulgent. That was the message my parents gave me as I was growing up. Anything I wanted for myself was always questionable. And that's the message you seem to be getting from your mother. I've found, however, that as I've worked through the fear, as I've recognized that the fear has to do with the past and is irrational in terms of the present, I've been a lot more comfortable doing things for myself. It's a wonderful freedom."

"I can't imagine not being afraid of my mother," Laura confesses. "I always know she's going to tear me down. And then I think I have to explain and justify myself to her, and then she comes back with more criticism. I end up feeling like she's mopped the floor with me. I can never win with her."

I explain that she'll be a lot less afraid as she begins to see her mother more realistically, rather than as the powerful figure of her childhood. Then I add: "There's something you could try. It has worked for me with a variety of people, and a friend of mine has used it with *her* mother to great effect. When your mother tells you that you're stupid and you've wasted money and why don't you ever get any sense, instead of making excuses, or trying to ignore her, or becoming whiney and angry, give it right back to her. For example, you could say: 'What kind of nonsense are you giving me? I never heard anything so silly as your telling me I shouldn't get dishes. I can't believe you're spouting such foolishness.' This way you're getting off the subject of dishes, and you're putting the responsibility right squarely on her. It's not *your* problem, as she's trying to make it, it's *her* problem, and she'd better deal with it. That kind of response can take the wind right out of her sails. You can do this with a lot of things, not just with the dishes. I think you'll be surprised at how it will change her reaction to you."

There's a general positive reaction to my illustration, and I go on to tell the group that I used that technique not too long ago with a relative of mine who asked me, for at least the tenth time, if I had a man in my life and was I ever going to get married again. The women groan. The question is a familiar one. "Instead of retorting, 'None of your business,' or instead of making a lot of excuses and explanations as I had in the past," I continue, "I looked him straight in the eye and said in my most amazed voice: 'I can't believe you're asking me such a question.' He got very confused and embarrassed and didn't seem to know what to say. He never asked me that question again."

The women love the story, and I go on to tell Laura that even if she uses this technique, she still has to explore why she continues to have such an involved relationship with her mother. What is she doing to perpetuate it? How can she change it?

Laura claims she understands that. "My shrink wants me to work on that, too," she explains. "I guess it's time I got with it."

"I think so, too," I say. "The problem won't go away by itself. In fact, if you don't deal with it, it will only get worse, more deeply ingrained."

"I know," Laura groans. "Life is hard."

I agree with her that it is, but I also tell her that it's a lot easier when all the irrational behavior doesn't get in the way. Laura says she hopes that's true, and I state that I know it's true from my own experience—that's precisely why I'm giving the workshop. She gives me her far-away look, and I can see that the subject is closed.

"We have only a short time left before the end of the session," I tell the women. "Are there any things you want to bring up before we stop?"

Julia says: "I feel that we've covered just about everything I've wanted to talk about. The five weeks have been very helpful."

"Only four for you," Laura reminds her.

Julia acknowledges her mistake.

"I've found the sessions helpful, too," Susan declares. "I've begun to mull over stuff I've never thought of before."

The other women claim they, too, have found new ideas through the workshop.

I say that I've enjoyed the five weeks immensely, that the group has been a pleasure to work with. I smile at them. They smile at me. And the time is up.

I think about the women as I walk uptown. I wonder if Elaine will actually go to a therapist. It's hard to tell. And even if she does go, will she make changes? I recall my therapist saying that one can make changes at any age if one really wants to. I'm not so sure Elaine wants to.

I'm sorry that Ann never revealed more about herself. Should I have tried to draw her out? I don't think so. She was free to say whatever she wanted to say, and she chose to be more of a helper, an advice-giver, than someone looking for suggestions.

It occurs to me that in the past two sessions Susan has been much less the helpless doll. She didn't give me the baby-blue-eyed stare once tonight. Not last week, either. Good for Susan. I remember Ann's offer of help to her and hope, once again, that Ann doesn't let Susan depend on her too much. I also hope Susan sticks with school. She's smart, and it would be a pity for her to go on trying to get by on her looks and on her cutesy behavior.

And what about Laura? Who knows! She was certainly
more responsive tonight, and she did buy the dishes. Buying
the dishes was a terrific assertion on her part. If she could
do that, she could do many other things. I wish I'd told her
so. But then I always walk away from a workshop wishing
I'd said half a dozen things, or berating myself because I've
neglected a certain topic. It's my old need to take care of
everything, to make everybody's life free of trouble and
anxiety. Since I can't do all that, no sense fretting over it.

I recall that in our initial session Connie maintained that
her big concern was finding less macho men, yet in subsequent sessions she talked about everything but men. Since
she's hardly shy, I have to assume she didn't feel there was
that much to discuss. And, I remind myself, we did talk at
length about relationships. Connie seemed to have gotten a
lot from the workshop. And she contributed so much—I
loved her story about going to a restaurant alone.

And how nice that Julia was able to give up her quest for
a new husband in favor of focusing on a new career. Well,
maybe she didn't give it up completely, but at least she's
dividing her attention somewhat.

Oh, dear! I suddenly realize how bereft I'm going to feel
next Thursday night when there's no workshop. But there
will be others, I remind myself, each one a slight variation
of the one before. That's what makes them so interesting:
all the different women with their own special concerns and
problems and ideas, and yet all of them so similar. And it
never ceases to amaze me that people can identify with my
experiences, can even benefit from them. I walk along feeling good, feeling warm. A moment later I notice with surprise that snow is falling. When did it start? Obviously I've
been deep in my own world, for I haven't the vaguest idea.

Chapter XI

We talked about love at the Haynes' last night. Leslie maintained that there is a great deal of love around, and I said there isn't. Her definition of love is to accept another person completely and to feel warmth and affection. I was unable to formulate my definition, but I think this is what I believe: A child loves naively, selfishly, spontaneously. An adult love implies unselfishness, a willingness to give up a part of oneself for the beloved person. An adult love to me is so profound that it can't be something one feels for a great many people, or indeed something one can easily feel for anyone.

—From my journal, February 4, 1961

As the years went by and I remained unmated, there were the inevitable queries about my love life. The questions always took me by surprise because they were frequently inserted in the middle of conversations that had absolutely no relevance to my personal relationships. It was as though our main discussion was merely a means of marking time before getting to the truly important subject. Thus, while deploring at length the depressing decrease of services in the city of New York, I would suddenly hear: "How's your social life?" Taken aback, I would answer, "Fine, I have some wonderful friends." The questioner would then look at me as though I were slightly dimwitted and would go on to explain that he or she was referring to my love life. Was I seeing *anyone in particular?*

No, I would reply. *I was not.* And what did that have to

do with the fact that public library branches were closing
down?

There were varied responses to my statement (the question of how my social life related to library closings was
ignored). Women often came back with the comment that
it was a pity there were so many fantastic women and so few
interesting men. "Men just haven't come up to the level of
women."

"I don't think that's the problem," I would reply. "It's
very difficult to have a close relationship."

Older people often expressed amazement that "such a
pretty girl" didn't have a man. I would then explain that being "pretty" (no sense going into the fact that at fifty I was
hardly a girl) had nothing to do with my having, or not having, an ongoing relationship with someone of the opposite
sex. The reason I didn't have a man in my life was because
I hadn't met anyone I cared about in "that way." I'm not at
all sure any of them believed me.

A divorced former dancer, whom I knew very slightly
from my neighborhood and who always seemed to be in the
depths of despair over the dissolution of a love affair, often
asked me how I could manage without a steady lover. "I'm
only happy if I have a man," she sadly confessed over and
over, her face a veritable tragedy mask. I refrained from
observing that her "happiness" had all the trappings of
misery and perhaps she ought to seek her pleasures elsewhere. But I did reply that I managed very well without a
lover and, in fact, was finding my life increasingly joyful.

Not that I didn't have relationships with men. I did. But
once I had split with Josh, and after having gone through
the eye-opening interchange with Steve, I found I was
much less insistent on keeping someone in my life who
would function as my permanent date.

Throughout 1977, I spent some pleasant evenings and
afternoons with Bruce, a divorced forty-seven-year-old man
who was a partner in an import-export business. When I

first started seeing Bruce, I was full of complaints and irritations. I loved going to bed with him, but I wasn't terribly interested in his ideas and opinions. He was intelligent, but he didn't read enough to suit me. He didn't always want to do the same things I liked to do. One Sunday he took me to the country to visit friends of his, and as usual all the components weren't completely to my liking: The people were nice but not scintillating; I wanted to go for a long walk while the others insisted on a sedentary afternoon; our hosts played music that wasn't to my taste.

"That day was such a letdown," I told my therapist. "All I really wanted to do was have a fabulous country walk with Bruce and then to go to bed with him. And instead I was forced to make small talk with the other people."

"Did you get to go to bed with Bruce?" she asked.

I smiled. "Yes, finally, at the end of the day. That was terrific."

"Why then must *everything* be exactly as you want it? Why couldn't you have enjoyed the day for what it was? The people were nice, the house was pleasant, and at the end of the day you and Bruce would make love. So what if the music wasn't your kind of music? Would it have been so terrible to give up a walk or to take a walk alone? By demanding perfection, you cheat yourself out of the pleasures that exist."

"You have a point," I conceded. "It's just that so many things about Bruce make it difficult for me to want to be involved with him."

Another challenge from my therapist: "Why does it always have to be an 'involvement?' Why can't Bruce be someone you see from time to time, with whom you enjoy having dinner or going to a movie, and with whom you enjoy making love? Every relationship doesn't have to be a huge commitment."

I thought about her words for several days. They made sense to me. They showed me that, despite the fact that I had lost the desperation to find a man, I hadn't lost the need to make the man in my orbit into a perfect parent. I was still demanding seamlessness, an absence of wrinkles, a constant blending and harmonizing. I wanted the impossible, and consequently I was always disappointed.

I began to reevaluate Bruce. As my therapist had said, he was someone I enjoyed sleeping with and going to movies and supper with. Come to think of it, how nice that he offered those few delights. Why was I focusing so much on what he didn't offer? Lord knows, I had plenty of friends with whom I could discuss books and music, and there was no dearth of soulmates willing to probe endlessly with me the painful complexity of the human condition. Did I need all that from Bruce?

Once I was able to accept Bruce just as he was, our relationship became infinitely simpler. We ate and made love and did a lot of window-shopping—the latter one of Bruce's favorite activities. At my suggestion, we spent a charmed summer day together at the Bronx Botanic Gardens. We hiked through that oasis of lush greenery that reminded me so much of Vermont, then sat by a waterfall that conjured up recollections of winding country roads and covered wooden bridges. It was hard to imagine that ugly city streets and dirty buildings were only minutes away. Later we spread out a blanket in a shady grove and feasted on cheese, strawberries, and chilled white wine. At the end of the afternoon, at Bruce's suggestion, we went to his apartment and made love, then showered and took off for the movies—*Annie Hall*; could we have made a better choice? We finished up our day eating hot pastrami sandwiches at the neighborhood delicatessen.

I have no idea if Bruce, whom I rarely see now, even remembers our afternoon and evening together, but it really doesn't matter. I recall it with great affection, and I probably always will.

There were memorable moments, as well as afternoons

and evenings, that might have passed me by during my days
of searching for perfect sharing. One occurred during a concert of arias from Bach cantatas that I attended with a
man who was about fifteen years my senior. His regular
companion had gotten sick at the last minute, and knowing
I liked music he had invited me in her place.

Now, this man and I had no particular relationship. We
were friends in passing, our conversation was generally
limited to pleasantries. He wasn't someone I was particularly at ease with. And yet during the concert, after the
alto, violin, and strings had performed a hauntingly beautiful aria from the *Passion According to St. Matthew*, we had
spontaneously turned toward one another, both with tears
in our eyes, and had smiled and wordlessly shaken our
heads at the wonder of it all. The moment had opened a
door, and during intermission we were easier, more relaxed
with each other. There was a new dimension to our relationship.

When I got home I thought: That moment is what sharing is all about. It can happen suddenly with almost anyone, if you let it. In the past I wouldn't have let it. I would
have been much too busy wishing I were with a younger
man, a man I cared for, a man who would fit into other
areas of my life. Of course I would have been moved by the
music, but I wouldn't have wanted to show my emotion to
someone I wasn't "involved with," and I wouldn't have been
at all interested in *his* feelings. I would have turned my
face in the opposite direction, and that lovely moment
would have been lost to me forever. How much fuller life
was when I didn't force and push and manipulate.

One afternoon in the spring of 1978 I was typing up an
article about an older woman-younger man relationship
when I found myself thinking back to a love affair I'd had
half my lifetime ago. I had been twenty-five, living alone
and working, while the man—Sam was his name—had been
twenty, a blond, handsome college student, still living with

his parents in Boston. We met in summer stock in New England, where I was the leading lady and he was an apprentice. We carried on passionately all summer and continued seeing each other in New York throughout the fall, winter, and spring when Sam would drive down from Boston on weekends. I think Sam viewed me as this worldly older woman, while I felt uneasy carrying on so with such a young kid. Our breakup, however, had nothing to do with age. It was simply typical of all my breakups of that period; the following summer I went off to a summer stock company in the Midwest and met another man. Via letter, I guiltily informed Sam that we were through. Two days after he received my note of rejection, Sam arrived at the stock company, determined to woo me back. But I was obdurate. I was in love, and as much as I liked Sam, last year's boyfriend was no match for this year's fresh new romance.

In the fall, Sam and I met a couple of times in New York for drinks and the shedding of a few tears over our lost passion, and then our paths ceased to cross.

Through the years I had heard from mutual friends that Sam still lived in Boston, was married to a beautiful woman —younger than himself—had two children, and was very successful as the head of his own public relations firm.

Now, sitting at my desk, I reflected on how nice it would be to talk to old Sam. I wondered how he looked after all the years—probably more handsome than ever. What was his life like up in Boston? Very glamorous and social, no doubt. I picked up the phone, dialed information, and got the number of Sam's business. A few minutes later I heard Sam's astonished voice, and then we were talking freely and excitedly as though twenty-five years had never passed.

My fantasies of Sam's life were certainly way off the mark. His existence was anything but glamorous and social. He was in the process of getting a painful divorce—"Funny you should call just as I'm splitting." His marriage had been

awful for a long time. He had developed a drinking problem. For the past five years he had let himself go in every
way: he had gotten fat, unhealthy, depressed, miserable.
Amazingly, however, he had kept a firm grip on the business, and it was thriving. The kids were great—a girl ten,
a boy twelve—but Sam's problems had taken their toll of
them, too.

"Now," Sam announced, "I'm trying to get myself together. I joined AA six months ago—haven't touched a drop
since—I'm going to the gym, I'm eating properly, I'm beginning to like myself."

Sam came to New York on business the following week
and took me to lunch. We met in the lobby of his hotel.
There he was, my young lover, with thinning, gray-blond
hair, deeply etched lines in his still handsome face, and a
noticeable roll of fat around his midsection—"I'm working
that off at the gym," he explained with some embarrassment. When he greeted me, Sam kissed me warmly and
sensually on the lips. He repeated the kiss several times, and
I was not unresponsive. On the way to lunch he kept his
arm lightly on my shoulders.

Like old times, I thought. How extraordinary that I
called when he was in the process of getting a divorce. Perhaps it was fate. As I listened to Sam over lunch—he sipping
Perrier, I sipping white wine—I figured it was more likely
plain coincidence. I could see Sam was struggling to get his
life together, much as I had struggled four and a half years
ago. With all his financial security, he still spoke of being
alone with awe and terror, and wondered aloud if he could
really hack it. On the other hand, he was proud of himself:
proud of giving up liquor, proud of making a stab at going
it alone. He wanted to know how I had managed. When did
the scared feelings go away? What could he do about loneliness? Several times during the meal he reached across the
table and took my hand. I didn't need my rational self to
point out that Sam was looking hungrily in all directions

for a perfect partner, and that, if I wanted, I could offer myself as a contender for the role with a pretty good chance of winning the dubious prize. I was quite sure I *didn't* want it. I had come too far for that.

What was fascinating to me was that, now that I was able to look beyond my own needs, I could truly enjoy Sam, for despite all his problems and fears, he was funny, bright, warm, good to be with. I was learning more about him during our two-hour lunch than I had learned in the year we had been lovers. At one point we talked about the 1960s, and I mentioned that I had been something of an anti-war activist. Sam laughed: "You always were gung-ho for liberal causes."

"Weren't you against the Vietnam war?" I asked.

"No. I was for it. That is, until we were losing. Then I thought we should get out."

I was shaken by his answer. "Weren't you against it on moral and ethical grounds?" I persisted.

Sam laughed again. "I was *for* it on moral and ethical grounds. I believed in the domino theory." I looked stunned, and Sam said: "You don't remember, do you? I was always politically conservative. You kept trying to convert me."

Conservative? I had gone with a conservative? How had that happened? No, I didn't remember. But then, I had probably been so involved in my attempts to change Sam that I had never bothered to listen to him. But why was I getting so worked up now? Didn't he have a right to his own opinions? Did our lunch have to become unpleasant because Sam and I disagreed politically? I smiled at him. "I won't try to convert you anymore. We can be friends and still have different points of view."

Sam also reminded me that he had been a male chauvinist, still was to some extent, although he *was* trying to shake off the old convictions—not so easy to do. On that issue, he claimed he was willing to be converted. Perhaps he was willing. I wasn't so sure.

We talked about Sam's drinking. "How did it start?" I asked.

"But I always drank. It just got worse as time went on. Don't you remember?" I shook my head. "You'd get high on one glass of wine, and I'd go on and on."

Was that how it was? Yes, I vaguely remembered. But it hadn't seemed so bad in those days. He had been just a crazy college kid boozing it up. Who knew then that he was in the process of building a habit that would do him in later on?

After lunch Sam walked me to the subway. Again he put his arm around my shoulders, and I, getting into the spirit of things, slipped my arm around his not-so-slim waist. Even with the added flesh, he felt good.

"We always did make a great-looking couple," Sam commented jubilantly.

"Oh, Sam," I protested. "Who cares about how we look?"

"I care," he declared indignantly. "For five years I let myself deteriorate. I didn't care how I looked. Now I care. I like it that I'm looking good again. I like it that we look good together."

"Okay," I replied. "The fact is, we're at different stages. I've spent so many years concerned with the externals that my goal is to get away from them. You want to get back to them. Let's face it, we're very different, separate, complex people."

Sam and I had two more lunch dates, and then I didn't hear from him for a few months. When he called, it was to tell me that he hadn't been in touch because he'd been involved with someone he'd met through AA and all his free time had been devoted to her. "We just broke up," he said. "We were both getting too clutchy, too jealous, too anxious. I can't take such an intense relationship right now. I've got to find someone who will sort of be there and make things easier for me."

I refrained from asking why he had to find someone, why he couldn't really try being alone for awhile. I knew why. He was scared to death. Instead, I asked how he was enjoying his bachelor apartment; at our last meeting he had mentioned he was having it decorated. He replied that he didn't spend much time there, that he usually became restless being alone. He then wondered if I'd like to come to Boston for a weekend.

Why not? I reasoned. After all, we know each other. We've been lovers. It would be fun having him show me Boston, eating together, sleeping together. It wouldn't be like spending a weekend with a stranger. "Sure," I answered. "I'd like that."

"How about this weekend?" I could hear the desperation in his voice. He wanted someone to assuage the loneliness of his empty apartment.

"I can't come this weekend, but I'll take a rain check."

"I guess it's a little last-minute." He sounded very disappointed. "I'll call you and we'll make a date."

After I hung up, it struck me that just because Sam and I had been lovers twenty-five years ago didn't make us intimates now. We weren't the same people anymore. I was no longer the insecure young woman trying to find self-esteem through a succession of admirers, and Sam was far removed from the starry-eyed college student who considered it a great adventure to sleep with an "older woman" in a narrow bed in her tenement apartment. Before talking of cozy weekends, we'd best get to know one another in the present. My instincts told me that Sam couldn't wait for that. He wanted satisfaction *now*. I could imagine him this very minute, frantically going through his little black book, searching for the magic someone to fill the looming void of Saturday and Sunday.

How clearly I could see Sam. And how much easier that

clarity made my life. I wasn't angry at Sam, and I didn't feel abandoned. I just knew, very realistically, exactly what I could expect. Had I been able to look at Stuart and Andrew and Josh, not to mention my former husband and my son, with such unclouded vision, I would have spared myself all those useless tears, anxieties, rages, and self-recriminations. What a relief to have them in the past. What a joy to be free.

As 1978 drew to a close, I was startled to note that I hadn't had an ongoing relationship with a man for many months. And then I had to acknowledge that maybe that was the way it would be the rest of my life. How did I feel about that? A little sad, perhaps, but certainly not morose. It would be nice to meet someone I cared for, and who cared for me, but I knew I couldn't count on it. And if it never happened, I could only hope that my work, my friends, my expanding activities would be enough.

There were occasions, however, when I was sure there could be no substitute for someone special, but even at those times I was able to work through the feeling and to prove myself wrong. New Year's Eve, 1978, was such a time. As a fifty-first birthday gift (fifty-one!), my writer friend, Cathy, presented me with two house seats for the New Year's Eve performance of the hit Broadway show, *Ain't Misbehavin'*. I had gasped at her extravagance—thirty dollars a ticket. Was I worth all that money? Did Cathy know what she was doing? Cathy assured me she did. She was thrilled to be able to give me such a present. My therapist's words from a recent session came back to me:

"It's time you allowed people to do things for you," she had counseled. "Everyone appreciates being able to give a gift, to do a favor. If you're the one who's always doing for others, you deprive your friends of a real pleasure."

So I kissed Cathy and expressed my deepest thanks and delight—the best birthday gift I'd ever received—and then anguished over whom I should take. There was no one special, and this was such a special event. How could I invite just a plain friend? My rational self was quick to tell me that this was indeed a special night, but it wasn't going to be the last one I'd ever have. It didn't have to be inflated beyond what it was. The person to ask was obviously my friend, Jack. He was a writer, had been a theater critic, had shared some theater-going experiences with me, and besides, I liked him; he was funny, nice, good company.

I argued that Jack probably had someone special he'd prefer to be with on New Year's Eve; he wouldn't want to spend the night with just a plain old friend. My rational self conceded that might be so, but I couldn't know definitely unless I asked.

Surprise! Jack had no plans; he accepted my invitation with almost as much enthusiasm as I had expressed when I received the tickets. It appeared I had made the right choice.

New Year's Eve started out auspiciously. Jack picked me up in his car, and when we arrived in the theater district we immediately found a parking place on the street—an almost miraculous happening in New York City. The show was a wonder: sexy, funny, sad, warm, brilliantly performed, and studded with all those incomparable Fats Waller songs. We never wanted it to end. Even the audience was terrific: the men and women around us were beautiful, marvelously dressed, and seemed to love the show as much as we did. They blended so perfectly with my mood that I suspected Cathy had hired them from Central Casting as part of my birthday present.

After the show, we drove uptown to a party given by friends of Jack's. This time we had parking troubles. Every garage was filled to capacity, and dozens of cars competed for the few empty spaces on the street. We cruised the area for three quarters of an hour, and I marveled at Jack's even temper as car after car cut in front of us to grab a coveted space. (A few months later, when Jack and I were going to the movies and having a similarly hard time parking, Jack became enraged and started swearing and yelling at other drivers. "Hey!" I said. "I thought you didn't get upset at parking difficulties." "What made you think that?" he wondered, snarling out another expletive. "You were so easy-going and pleasant New Year's Eve, and we were having much more trouble than tonight." "But that was different," Jack had responded. "That was a special night. I wasn't going to spoil it by losing my temper." I had never considered such a possibility. I had never imagined he might have cared about the evening as much as I had. But he had. He had been my collaborator and I hadn't even known it.)

The New Year's Eve party, while not as spectacular as the show, was equally as successful. There were lots of friendly people—if anyone was scintillating, I didn't know and I couldn't have cared less—and plenty of free-flowing champagne. We talked and drank, and at midnight there were kisses and good wishes all around. Then we went to the large windows that overlooked Central Park and watched the traditional display of fireworks.

What a fitting way to end and start a year, I thought, as hundreds of rockets soared over the trees, high up into the sky, where they burst into clusters of brilliant sapphire-blue, ruby-red, emerald-green, and golden stars. I felt Jack's arm encircle my waist, and I leaned my head contentedly on his shoulder. Together we watched the stars blaze boldly for a brief moment, then slowly fade, only to be replaced by still more breathtaking, jewel-like explosions.

I couldn't remember a happier New Year's Eve. At that moment, I wanted nothing more than to be in that particular room, with those particular people and with my friend, Jack, at my side. How lucky I was!

As ever, my rational self had to have the last word: Not lucky. It's not just that good fortune has smiled on you. You've helped make the evening joyful by bringing all your good feelings to it. And you've earned those feelings. You've worked with great diligence to uncover them. You've spent five years getting rid of the clutter that stood in their way. You've made your own good luck. Give yourself a little credit.

I smiled to myself and regretfully watched the last flash of color fade from the sky. Yes, it was true. I had worked hard, very hard. I sighed deeply, gratefully. Ah! How lucky I was that all the work was actually paying off.

Chapter XII

I've been putting off writing in my journal because I haven't known what's been happening to me. Last night I felt like tearing myself apart, like jumping from a window, like screaming, and I said to my husband, "I've got 'the sickness unto death.'" And I do. I have no faith in the future. I go through each day automatically, with no belief that anything good will ever happen. I am very frightened of this period of my life. I become afraid that I shall always be like this. Afraid that I shall say each day, "What's to become of my life?" until there is nothing left to do but die.
—From my journal, February 1, 1960

I had thought to end my book with New Year's Eve, 1978. It seemed a natural: rockets bursting in air, my head resting comfortably on Jack's shoulder, surrounded by warm, friendly people. But when 1979 presented me with an opportunity to begin to move physically, as well as emotionally, away from my moorings, I wanted to include the experience.

Although the first five years after the dissolution of my marriage were marked by continual changes in attitudes and behaviors, they were also remarkable in that I stayed very close to home and my rocking chair. My activities were largely confined to Manhattan Island and its surrounding areas, and it was a rare occasion when I ventured far afield. Over the many months, there had been two sojourns to New Hampshire—both two-day visits to my son at camp, approximately eight weekends with friends in their beach and country homes, and the one weekend in Nantucket with Andrew.

Each year I promised myself a vacation, and each year I gave myself a dozen reasons why getting away would be out of the question: I couldn't leave my son alone; money was needed for my son's camp; my son must have a new bicycle and money for a camping trip; there were private school payments I had to meet; I didn't feel I could leave my work for more than a couple of days. All those reasons were absolutely valid, but they also covered up my fear of giving myself something pleasurable, of denying my son anything—he could very well have earned the money to buy his bicycle, and, in fact, he could have worked that summer instead of going camping. They also obscured the real terror I felt that should I go away for any length of time, I'd come back to find my whole world gone, ruined, irretrievable.

Throughout the years, I dreamed of a trip to London; actually, I had been dreaming of London as long as I could remember. I had never been there—had never been anywhere in Europe—and I wanted to see it more than any city I could think of. I had always been a pushover for British films and had devoutly wished that, like the movie characters, I could roam those historic London streets, explore the Tate and the British Museum, go to the theater every night, stop for a snack in a pub, ride the underground, take a train to the country. But instead of planning for such a vacation, I watched friends fly back and forth, as nonchalantly as I might shuttle between New York and Boston, and promised myself that sooner or later my turn would come.

By the end of 1978, I began to feel that my turn had better come sooner. I needed a change. I was choking on the daily routine of earning a living and being a parent. It had been a hard year: I had dealt with some tough challenges from my son, and I had worked without a break for eight months, pushing to finish the last of my collaborative ventures. For the first time since that January morning in 1974, I felt bone-weary, truly exhausted from the never-ending struggle simply to survive. There had to be more to life than that.

At the beginning of 1979, I made the ritual resolve—this year, London—then forgot about it. But in February, when my friend, Cathy, announced that she and Nicholas, the man she lived with, would take a house in London for June, July, and August, I confronted the tantalizing possibility of being Cathy's and Nicholas' houseguest for a couple of weeks.

"Maybe I'll fly over and visit you," I casually suggested as Cathy and I were having lunch.

"You know you're always welcome." Her voice was flat, her eyes skeptical. Having watched me fruitlessly go through my I'm going-to-London routine many times in the past, she was not about to register great enthusiasm. She'd believe me when I had my plane ticket and passport. She was quite right to be skeptical. Five minutes later I had dismissed the idea with my usual army of excuses: my apartment was going co-op, school tuition had gone up, my son needed new clothes, the refrigerator should be replaced.

And then, a month later, a thirty-two-year-old woman friend of Cathy's died, and all my excuses paled in the face of life and death. The woman's name was Paula, and she had been a singer. Cathy and Nicholas invited friends of Paula's to an informal memorial brunch in her honor—"Paula wouldn't have wanted anything somber," Cathy told me, explaining the brunch. "She would have wanted everyone to remember her while having fun and eating good food."

It was very simple and beautiful. One friend played Robert Schumann's *Widmung* (Dedication) on the piano, and another spoke about his friendship with Paula. But the last and most moving statement came from Paula herself, for Nicholas ended the service by playing some tapes of

Paula singing. Her extraordinary voice, that could soar and swoop, turn and quiver, be sexy or funny or achingly sad, filled the room. She sang of love and heartbreak and delicious, sensual feelings, and wanting a room somewhere with an enormous chair, and knowing her lover was nearer to her than the wind is to the willow. On and on she sang, and everyone in the room wept.

Except the tears weren't only for the untimely loss of Paula. We also wept over an unrealized life. We shed bitter tears over the fact that that glorious voice, a voice that could hold its own with the voices of Streisand and Garland, had rarely been heard outside of someone's living room. For the seven years I had known her, Paula had talked wistfully, angrily, determinedly of getting her act together, of taking a chance, of moving forward. But she never had. Even when there had been offers and interest from the professional world, she had held back in fear. She had been so imprisoned by the unresolved conflicts from her past that she could never find the strength to break free, could never let her life take off as her voice had done so many times. And now it was too late.

When the tapes ended, I went into the bedroom to get a tissue, and there was Cathy, crying and blowing her nose. She looked at me helplessly, her eyes red-rimmed and watery. "What was the point of her death?" she asked in a tired, bewildered voice. "What was the point of her life? She accomplished nothing: she had that absolutely gorgeous voice and all that musical talent, and she did nothing with them; she wanted children and never had them; her parents were so destructive to her, yet she clung to them. I can't understand what meaning her life and death had."

I shook my head. "I don't know that life and death are ever very reasonable and logical," I replied sadly. "But I do know that her death has had meaning for me. Suddenly, listening to those tapes, it became so clear to me that life can't be postponed. No matter how frightened we are, we

have to use the precious time given to us. We have to! There
are no second chances!" I reached out and touched Cathy's
hand. "I'm coming to visit you in London this summer,
Cathy. I'm not going to put it off any longer. I must finally
make this trip."

"Oh, yes! You must!" Cathy exclaimed passionately through
her tears. And then we hugged each other and laughed and
cried, and Cathy said: "Tell me when! What date will you
come?"

Without a moment's hesitation I replied: "August 15. I
first came to New York on August 15, and that was one of
the best things I ever did. So that's the date I'll come to
London. And I'll stay two weeks."

The following day I called a travel-agent friend and
ordered a ticket. "The least expensive flight you can get me,"
I pleaded.

"I'm so happy for you that you're finally going. Don't
worry. I'll get the best flight possible for the least amount
of money."

A few friends argued that I should take a standby flight:
"Why pay extra money? That's just plain foolish." But I
maintained that, although I was generally inclined toward
frugality, in this case—my first trip abroad—I wanted to go
in some kind of style. I was traveling at the height of the
season, and there were sure to be mobs of people "standing
by." I didn't want to have to worry about the possibility of
not getting a seat. I would (gulp) pay the extra hundred
dollars for peace of mind.

One woman, who had no idea what a momentous step this
trip was for me, made a face when I mentioned London
in August. "I was there last year and it did nothing but
rain," she had gloomily informed me. "Why not go some-
place warm and sunny?" She couldn't possibly understand
that I didn't mind the rain—it always rained in British films
—that I wasn't looking for sun and warmth. I wanted to see
London. I would take my umbrella and raincoat, and rain

or shine I'd walk all over the city; I would be the quintessential tourist. Drizzles would only add to the glamour.

"What a shame you can't stay longer than two weeks," was another comment. Little did that person know that two weeks sounded sinfully long to someone who, for five years, had never been away beyond two days.

Several people wondered where I would leave my son, and I always explained that he was seventeen, six months away from eighteen, and that I would leave him home to care for himself. I received a number of raised eyebrows, but I wasn't fazed. I knew I could leave him. In the past, I had worried about how responsible he'd be: Would he eat properly? Would he and his friends mess up the house? Would precious possessions get broken? Now I was willing to take a risk. If he didn't eat properly for two weeks, he wouldn't perish; should the house get messy it could be tidied; and I wasn't going to stay home forever to guard my possessions—I would survive a few broken objects.

Not once was I swayed by outside dark predictions and words of caution, but I *was* thrown by the surfacing of my own irrationalities. They came to light when I received the bill for the plane fare. That innocuous, oblong piece of paper, with the figure $400 printed on it, momentarily transformed me from the confident woman in charge of her life to a quivering mass of indecision: the old band started tightening across my chest; I could barely get my breath; I was drenched in perspiration; my legs fairly buckled beneath me. My God! What was I doing? These were inflationary times! Even though I was earning more money, it was not worth a penny more than what I'd earned three years ago! How could I indulge myself at a time like this? How dare I behave so extravagantly? How dare I go on a trip when I needed a new refrigerator? When, a day later, my bedroom air conditioner stopped functioning, necessitating a sizable repair, I was ready to cancel the reservation.

It was then that my rational self reminded me of Paula. And once more I was back in Cathy's and Nicholas' living room, listening to that magnificent voice that Paula, with all her excuses and terrors, had kept closeted for an entire lifetime. No! That was not what I wanted for myself. Yes, these were inflationary times, but if I waited another year prices could very well become even more inflated. Airplane fares were at their lowest now, they would surely be higher in 1980. And wasn't I saving money by staying with Cathy and Nicholas? When would I ever again have such an opportunity? What huge extravagance was I talking about? Last year, without batting an eyelash, I had plunked down six hundred dollars for my son's summer vacation—and he hadn't even enjoyed himself. Now I was falling apart over a four hundred dollar round-trip plane fare. Was I crazy? I couldn't turn back. I had to move forward. Who knew what next year would bring? I could live another year with the old refrigerator.

Next, I recalled that I had gotten the stereo with fear and trembling, and nothing terrible had happened; I had bought my son his beautiful chair, and the sky hadn't fallen on my head; and last year I had had the temerity to slipcover the couch and to reupholster the chair and hassock, and I had continued to live on unscathed. I was sure to survive the trip. No! Not just survive; I would thrive on it.

As I write these final pages, it is the beginning of June. The air is muggy, heavy, polluted. It will be a hot, uncomfortable summer. But for once I don't anticipate the coming tropical months with dread. I look forward to them. I have my ticket—all paid for; I have my passport. I am very excited.

Last week, a man I know came up with the suggestion that while in London I should "pop over to Paris." He had insisted that it would be a shame to be in Europe and not see Paris. I had patiently explained that I didn't want to make a frantic trip. I just wanted to see London and perhaps some of the English countryside. I'd get to Paris during another trip.

"It's just such a pity to miss that wonderful city," he had persisted. "I'm sure you could squeeze it in."

"No," I had replied, again with great patience. "My goal is not to 'squeeze' something in. I want to explore one city thoroughly. Getting to know London will be a long-time dream come true. I couldn't ask for more. After all," I added, my voice strong and resonant, "I'm sure this isn't going to be my last trip to Europe. I'm positive I'll go many more times—to other places, as well. There is so much in the world I want to see and find out about, and possibly even write about. Now that I've made the first step, nothing can hold me back."